OSTIA ANTICA

GUIDE TO THE EXCAVATIONS

by Angelo Pellegrino

This book was edited and published by
A.BE.T.E. spa, via Prenestina 685
00155 Rome - Tel. +39 0622 5821
ISBN 88-7047-091-1

Editing
Stefania Spirito

Translation
Oona Smyth

Graphics
E. B. Design

Maps
Alberto Duelli

Colour separations
La Cromografica - Rome

Photographic references
Soprintendenza Archeologica di Ostia Archive (including some pictures from the National Geographic)
Editorial Museum Archive
"Il Dagherrotipo" Archive
The excavational plan is taken from the book Ostia, Armando Editore

A.BE.T.E. spa is at the complete disposal of those with rights regarding unidentified sources of images.

CONTENTS

EXCAVATIONAL PLAN

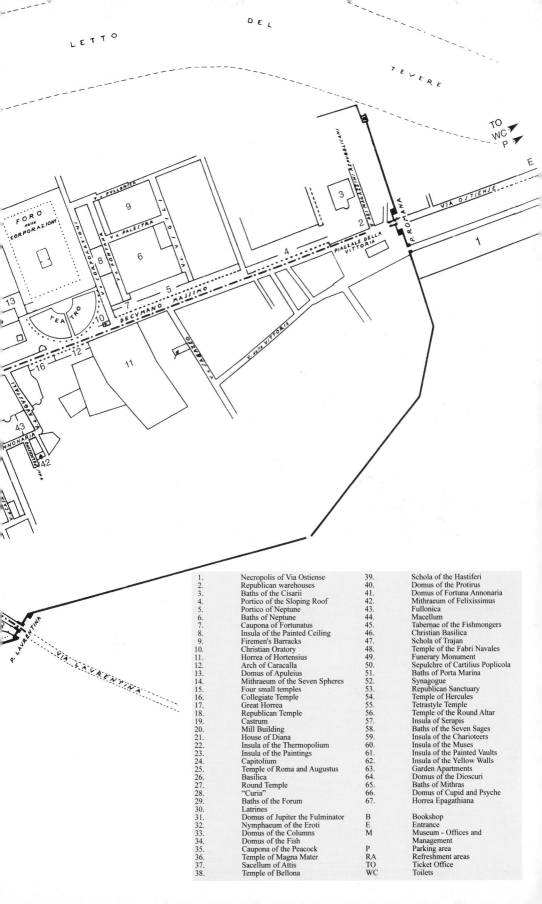

The morphology of the site

The current geo-territorial conformation of the Ostia area differs from its configuration during ancient times and during the Republican and Imperial ages. Formed during the previous two millennia from the deposits left by the river and by the numerous changes in the Tiber's course, the sandy alluvial land near the river-mouth contained many water tables.

Two main aspects distinguish the modern landscape of Ostia with respect to that of ancient times: the course of the Tiber and the coastline. As far as the former is concerned, in ancient times, after describing an almost right-angled meander, the river ran along the northern side of Ostia before flowing into the sea. Today the river flows alongside the western sector of the city for a brief stretch, following the down-hill displacement of its bed brought about by the famous, disastrous flood of 1557. The second difference concerns the coastline, which is currently separated from the ancient ruins by approximately four kilometres of terra firma (on which the modern settlement of "Ostia Lido" has been built), created by the debris left by the river during the last two thousand years.
When we realise that Ostia was a city built by the sea and by the river, it is not hard to understand how, during the centuries, its position endowed it with both military and strategic importance as well as economic power.

The earliest times

Historical sources from the Republican Age right up to the early Middle Ages agree that Ostia was founded by the fourth Roman king, Ancus Marcius, presumably around 620 B.C.

The primary motive for this choice of location lay in the opportunity of exploiting the salt pans at the mouth of the Tiber, whose importance in the ancient world was obviously considerable. On the other hand, the name of the city derives from the word *ostium* (river mouth) and clearly refers to the Tiber. But it is likely that other economic and political motivations were not lacking.

These include the need to control the lower valley of the Tiber both commercially – given that this waterway represented the main communication channel between the coast and the inland – as well as strategically, given the Etruscan presence on the other bank of the river.

Unfortunately, the still fragmentary nature of the archaeological evidence regarding this ancient phase of Ostia's existence makes it impossible to establish with any certainty the precise location of the royal settlement (although there are no longer any real doubts about the fact that it really existed). The most likely location is by the mouth of the Tiber, on an ancient road axis coming from the Laurentine region. In historic times, its route was followed by the 'Via della Foce' (road of the river mouth) which passed through the inhabited area of Ostia. But we cannot exclude the hypothesis that it was located in the area corresponding to the medieval town of Gregoriopolis, the highest site in this part of the territory and where a number of pieces of ancient pottery have been found, albeit during unofficial excavations. The occasional references made to the town by historical sources in the context of marginal 5th-century events do however indirectly confirm its antiquity.

The Republican Period

Archaeological documentation pertaining to the more ancient phases of Ostia's existence only become unequivocal from the beginning of the 4th century B.C. onwards. In 396 B.C. the Romans conquered Veii, and shortly afterwards, to consolidate their domain in the lower valley of the Tiber, they built a fortalice near the river mouth, conventionally (although incorrectly) defined as *castrum*. The camp was intended to defend the coast which was threatened by the maritime incursions of the Greeks and, above all, of the Syracusans, responsible for the terrible sack of the nearby Pyrgi in 384 B.C.. The *castrum* is generally considered be the first Roman colony, although the first true colonial foundation dates to several decades after the construction of the fortalice at the mouth of the Tiber. During the middle of the Republican period the military function prevailed and, from 267 B.C. onwards, one of the *quaestores* of the fleet was stationed at Ostia, which, as we know, became the main naval base during the Punic Wars, playing an important role in the campaign against Hannibal. After Rome had obtained the domination of the Mediterranean, during the latter half of the 2nd century B.C., the colony naturally began to assume a more commercial role. The old fortified settlement was abandoned, and numerous shops were built onto it for the storage and sale of the goods that were unloaded at the river port, which historical sources inform us also included grain.

Although the river port has yet to be uncovered, it undoubtedly extended along the northern edge of the settlement of Ostia, which was flanked by the left bank of the river along its whole length in Roman times. Furthermore, the port area faced the narrow strip of land bordered by the former meander of the Tiber. Recent investigations have documented the presence of a trans-Tiberine quarter, known as "Trastevere ostiense" ('Trastevere' means 'trans-Tiberine'), where warehouses and structures linked to river navigation jostled for space, giving the area its strongly commercial vocation.

It is likely that during the first half of the last century of the Republican period walls in *opus incertum* were built along three sides of the city (the northern side was bordered by the Tiber). The built-up area,

which had long since expanded beyond the enclosure of the *castrum*, was crossed by two main road axes, the *Cardo Maximus* and the *Decumanus Maximus*. Once it had reached the western side of the city, the latter, which was the urban continuation of the Via *Ostiensis*, divided, one branch going towards the mouth of the Tiber ("Via della Foce") and the other towards the beach: this fork was the urbanistic reflection of the two elements that had determined the birth, growth and prosperity of Ostia, that is, the river and the sea.

Other events affected the colony during the 1st century B.C. In 87 B.C., during the civil war, it was occupied and plundered by Marius; in 67 B.C., it was attacked by Cilician pirates who also destroyed the fleet moored by the mouth of the Tiber, an episode deplored by Cicero.

The Imperial Age

At the beginning of the Imperial age, it was considered necessary to endow this stretch of coast with a real sea port. The volume of sea trade handled by the capital had by now exceeded the capacity of the modest river-port structures, which could no longer provide an adequate refuge for the ships. Furthermore, the lack of a natural bay near the river mouth made it extremely difficult to pilot the ships into the river, especially in poor weather conditions. It also complicated the process of unloading cargo from the larger vessels (whose bulk prevented them from travelling upriver) onto

Museum of Ostia, terracotta architectural elements from the *Castrum* area (above). **The Decumanus by the Theater** (previous page)**. From the Hall of the Grain Measurers** (right)**. Capitolium** (following page).

the smaller river boats transporting it on to Ostia or Rome.

Although the project for a sea port was conceived by Caesar or maybe also by Augustus, it was not until A.D. 42 that it was actually carried out under Emperor Claudius who wished to build the complex two miles north of the Tiber mouth, corresponding to an area that is now Fiumicino, near the Leonardo da Vinci airport. However, the work immediately proved to have major technical shortcomings. In fact, its failure to provide a safe shelter for moored ships (due in part to the huge dimensions of the dock) caused Emperor Trajan to have a second dock built, probably between A.D. 106 and A.D. 113. This hexagonal-shaped dock was located further inland and was therefore more protected, and linked to Claudius' port via an artificial channel (corresponding to the current Fiumicino Canal).

Originally built as a port facility, the complex gradually turned into a town which, from the second half of the 3rd century A.D. onwards, began to replace Ostia as the focal point of sea trade and functioned as the main storage and clearing centre for goods headed for Rome. Its status was such that under Constantine it obtained civic administrative autonomy.

Nevertheless, the construction of the port and the resulting transfer of many commercial activities to the new port pole did not bring about, at least until the beginning of the 3rd century A.D., any social-economic or urbanistic decline in Ostia. On the contrary, the town's importance increased to the extent that the development of its existing administrative and commercial structures became necessary, given that these had yet to be created within the new port facility. On the other hand, it is obvious that it would take time for the new port (the biggest in the Mediterranean) to be organised efficiently and supplied with the whole range of services linked to commercial activities, like, for example, warehouses for the storage of goods, administrative offices for the control of food provisions or even the simple but indispensable commercial offices.

Around the middle of the 2nd century A.D. Ostia became a flourishing densely-populated centre (possibly around 50,000 inhabitants) mainly visited by merchants, travellers, shipowners, and craftsmen. The economic and commercial activities directly or indirectly conditioned by the presence of the imperial ports inevitably favoured the rise of a new clerical and commercial middle class also reflected by the town's development in architectural and town-planning terms.

The first step involved the building of a new forum – which had previously only existed on a very modest scale – with the reconstruction of the *Capitolium* (A.D. 120) followed by new baths, granaries, luxurious headquarters for trade associations and enormous tenement blocks. Whole town quarters were planned using a town-planning scheme. The Piazzale delle Corporazioni, or Square of the Guilds was monumentalised, soon becoming a focal point for those importing goods from the provinces.

The final major works carried out in Ostia date to the Severan dynasty and their marked interest in strengthening sea trade. The theatre was extended and a monumental honorary arch was built by its entrance on the Decumanus. The main work, however, involved the construction of the Via Severana linking Ostia and the port of Terracina. The commercial nature of the Square of the Guilds was accentuated by the creation of offices reserved for shipowners and commercial operators to advertise their commercial activities.

Nevertheless, Ostia's decline began halfway through the 3rd century A.D. brought about by the political and economic crisis that had hit the entire empire as well as by the importance assumed by Portus, to which all commercial activities had been transferred. The town had lost its economic lifeblood as shown by the abandonment of most of the *horrea,* the *insulae* and some prominent buildings, such as the Barracks of the Firemen whose main duty was to protect the granaries from fires. But emblematic of the crisis was the abandonment of the complex that had represented Ostia's economic and commercial prosperity for over one century: the Square of the Guilds.

Not only were no more statues erected in honour of local notables (generally involved in commercial activities) but, when around A.D. 350, it became necessary to restore the theatre, the breaks in the walls were filled in using the inscribed bases of the statues of the square.

Ostia practically became a residential centre whose housing no longer consisted of the densely-inhabited tenement blocks but was formed of low refined *domus*, set apart in gardens with nymphaea.

It often became necessary to knock down the previous *tabernae* in order to build these houses, a sign of the serious and irreversible crisis affecting the trade sector.
However, it would be misleading to imagine a city in a state of semi-abandonment.

In fact, during the course of the 4th century A.D., the Prefects of the Annona (food supplies) had a number of the most important buildings restored.

In addition to the works carried out to the theatre, described above, we should mention the Baths of the Forum, the largest and most important baths, which underwent partial restoration under the Prefect Ragonius Vincentius Celsus (A.D. 385-389).

Moreover, the extra-urban quarter outside Porta Marina continued to flourish thanks to the presence of the Via Severana which was the coast's main trade link to Portus.

Nevertheless, from the beginning of the 5th century A.D. onwards, the city underwent its definitive decline, recalled by the poet Rutilius Namatianus in all its desolation.

Halfway through the 6th century A.D., the writer Procopius described an Ostia in decline, totally cut off due to the obstacles impeding navigation of the Tiber and the totally overgrown Via Ostiense.

the NECROPOLIS of VIA OSTIENSE or of PORTA ROMANA

You enter the archaeological zone by walking up the avenue which takes you from Via dei Romagnoli (next to the castle of Julius the Second) straight to the ticket-office. After you have passed through the entrance, you will come upon a stretch of road paved with basalt blocks belonging to the Via Ostiense, the main artery linking Rome to Ostia from the Republican age onwards. The road is lined by unbroken rows of simple tombs and monumental sepulchres forming the city's oldest and most imposing burial ground. The structures in the necropolis, which was used from the 1st century B.C. until the late Imperial age, are so densely superimposed that it is no easy task to read the inscriptions of the single monuments. The tombs were built outside the inhabited area in accordance with an ancient rule, already known in the Greek world and contained in the Twelve Tables drawn up in Rome at the beginning of the 5th century B.C which forbade burial within a settlement. The tombs were originally concentrated on the southern side of the *Via Ostiensis* in compliance with an order issued by the Praetor *C.*

The Via Ostiense beyond Porta Romana.

Caninius during 150-80 B.C. forbidding the construction of private buildings in the strip of land near the Tiber, an area considered public property, so as not to interfer with the carrying out of the river port activities. The text of this ordinance is repeated on a series of cippi, uncovered along the northern sector of the town, one of which is close to the nearby gate through which the Via Ostiense passed to enter the settlement: *C(aius). Caninius C(ai) f(ilius) / pr(aetor) urb(anus) / de sen(atus) sent(entia) / poplic(om)*

ioudic(avit) ["Caius Caninius, son of Caius, town magistrate, by decision of the Senate allots (this area) to public use"]. Towards the end of the 1st century B.C., the necropolis extended slightly southwards, along either side of a beaten dirt road running through it; finally, at the height of the Imperial age, the last major group of tombs was formed even further south of the previous clusters, making it necessary to pave another road parallel to the Via Ostiense, conventionally called the "Via dei Sepolcri" (road of the sepulchres).

The most interesting sepulchre on this side of the road is the so-called **Tomb of Hermogenes**, built during the 2nd century A.D. on top of an existing construction, the circular tufa base of which can still be distinguished. The epigraph commemorates *C. Domitius Hermogenes*, who belonged to the *eques Romanus* (the equestrian order) and was the secretary (*scriba*) to the magistrates whose duties included the care of temples, public building and markets, and the supervision of public games (*aediles*) as well as decurion and *flamen*, that is a priest of the deified Hadrian. In recognition of his good works towards the city of Ostia, he had the honour of a funeral at public expense (rendered even more sumptuous by the use of the exotic and costly incense) and of an equestrian statue dedicated to him in the forum. Leaving Via Ostiense and

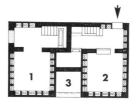

Fig. 1. Tomb of the 'Twin Columbaria'. 1 and 2 Columbaria; 3 *ustrinum*.

taking the Via di Ermogene, we enter the road of the sepulchres in order to visit the tombs on the northern side.

We should mention **Tomb No. 17**, also known as the Tomb "of the Small Arches" ("degli Archetti"), which you enter by going down a couple of steps. The tomb is a columbarium built in *opus reticulatum* with brick inserts at the beginning of the 1st century A.D., distinguished by the beautiful polychrome architectural decorations of the rear external wall. Still in an easterly position, slightly to the left of the above tomb, you will find **Tomb No. 20**,

also known as the "Twin Columbaria" ("Colombari Gemelli") because it is formed of two vaults with the same floor plan (Fig. 1), built during the same period (first half of the 1st century A.D.) and sharing a common rectangular room in the centre (*ustrinum*) which was the area occupied by the pyre during cremation. On the opposite side of the road, the impressive **Sarcophagus of Carminius Parthenopeus** (2nd century A.D.) towers over us on a travertine base. The inscription on the front side recalls the offices held by the deceased: *Sex. Carminius Parthenopeus* of equestrian rank was the decurion of the city of Ostia and also the head (*quinquennalis*) of the powerful builders' guild (*fabri tignuarii*). The route is completed by walking back up Via dei Sepolcri and Via di Ermogene to the area in front of Porta Romana.

Sarcophagus of Carminius Parthenopeus.

FUNERARY RITES AND MONUMENTS

The century-long use of the necropolis meant that various types of funeral rite and sepulchre alternated from the Republican age to the late Empire: a) from the end of the 1st century B.C. - beginning of the 1st century A.D., cremation was prevalently used. The sepulchres consist of open-roofed enclosures (the funerary urns containing the ashes of the dead person were stored below the floor) or by funeral monuments in the form of altar or *tholos*; b) in the 1st century A.D., cremation was still popular but the practice of burial began to spread. During this period the most widespread sepulchre was the columbarium, a vault with wall recesses containing the urns with ashes; c) from the 2nd-3rd centuries A.D., the practice of burial replaced other forms of funerary rite. The tombs were vaults containing marble or terracotta sarcophagi. There were often more modest burials where the dead were laid on shelves below the floor.

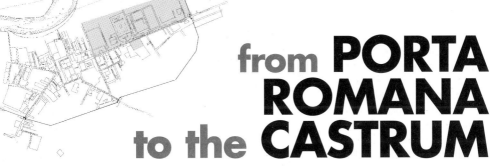

from PORTA ROMANA to the CASTRUM

This is the end of the extra-urban stretch of the Via Ostiense which entered the city through the so-called Porta Romana. Just before the city wall on the right you'll see the marble **Basis of Salus Augusta** (Basamento della Salus Augusta) supporting a statue dedicated to the Health (or safety) of the emperor and bearing the following inscription: *Saluti Caesaris August(i) / Glabrio patronus coloniae / D(onum) d(edit) f(aciendum) c(uravit)* ["In honour of the Health of Caesar Augustus, Glabrio patron of the colony presented (this statue) and ensured its erection"].

The donor can be identified as Manius Acilius Glabrius, member of the family of the *Acilii*, one of Ostia's oldest and most prominent families and major local landowners; towards the end of the 1st century A.D., he had this statue set up to commemorate the Emperor's visit to Ostia.

It should be pointed out that the *gens Acilia* had always been devoted followers of the cult of this divinity. So much so that in Republican times (54 B.C.) they had *denarii* minted with *Valetudo* (from *valere*= to

feel well) stamped on the front.

Facing the visitor is the external side of the **Republican Wall** surrounding the settlement with a nearly 1800-metre-long perimeter on three sides, the northern side being flanked by the Tiber. Built of imposing masonry in *opus quasi-reticulatum*, it was previously dated to the Sullan period, although researchers agree that there is no hard evidence for this dating; recent studies have proposed a more recent foundation date, around the middle of the 1st century B.C. Set into the wall is the so-called **Porta Romana**, the city entrance. Flanked by two square towers and formed of two spaces separated by tufa pillars, it originally had a vaulted roof with three fornices, or arched entrances; the two anterior pillars forming the jamb, still bear the grooves for the shutter. The remains of the gate are located below the Imperial age level which corresponded to the current basalt paving of the Via Ostiense. During a later phase, at the end of the 1st century A.D., when the road surface was raised, the gate was embellished with marble decorations, some of

Statue of Minerva.

which have been attached to a reconstructed wall inside.

Going through the gate, we find ourselves in a wide stretch of road known as **Piazzale della Minerva** following the discovery of a winged Minerva set on a high plinth. The statue depicts the goddess wearing a helmet and peplos, and holding a round shield in her right hand; traditionally dated to the Domitian period, the latest studies place it in the Republican age (around 60 B.C.) and suggest it may have been relocated at the end of the 1st century A.D. to decorate the upper section of the gate. Further ahead, on the left, you can see the remains of a **nymphaeum** from the late Imperial age which served as a drinking trough for the carters' horses whose journeys ended here at the city gate.

Opposite the statue, set into a modern wall are fragments of two identical **inscriptions** originally located inside and outside the attic of the gate. The recently retranslated text practically synthesises the history of the gate and the walls: decreed by the Senate and the Roman People for the colony of Ostia, the construction of the walls was begun by Cicero during the year of the consulate (63 B.C.) and they were completed, five years later, by Clodius Pulcher Pulcrus, his arch-enemy. Over a hundred years later, the gate, which had suffered the effects of time, was restored in monumental form, with marble decorations and the addition of the statue described above.

On the right-hand side of the square are the **Republican warehouses** (Magazzini Repubblicani) which originally consisted of a rectangular building in opus *quasi-reticulatum* surrounded by an portico with tufa pillars. The transformations undergone by the building in the following centuries make it hard to distinguish the original floor plan. The complex, which dates to the 1st century B.C., housed activities linked to the nearby river port, but

Baths of the Cisiarii, mosaic.

underwent modifications during the course of the Imperial age.

New buildings, not necessarily commercial in character, were built, the most noteworthy being the **Baths of the Cisiarii** (Terme dei Cisiarii) which supposedly belonged to the guild of the carters (*cisiarii*). Built under Hadrian, the baths underwent renovation on more than one occasion during the 3rd century A.D. The service areas are located along the eastern side, while two small heated rooms and figurative mosaic pavements are situated in the centre. But the most interesting mosaic is undoubtedly the one in the *frigidarium*, in the northern wing, depicting two

boundary walls, one running around the edge of the room and the other in the centre, between which various maritime or everyday scenes are taking place. Particularly worthy of interest is the lively representation of two-wheeled carts pulled by mules (*cisia* in Latin, giving the building its name) with drivers and travellers at various stages of their journeys. There are also light-hearted inscriptions containing the nicknames of the mules: *pudes* (prudish), *podagrosus* (gouty) and *barosus* (effeminate).

You now return to the square and walk along the **Decumanus Maximus**, the main road which ran from east to west dividing the city

Stretch of the Decumanus Maximus.

into two practically equal parts; the road was intersected by other perpendicular axes, called *cardines*, running from north to south. Ostia's Decumanus Maximus is very wide (around 9 m) allowing traffic to flow in both directions. A one-and-a-half-kilometre-long stretch linked Porta Romana with the gate known as Porta Marina near the ancient beach. Frequent floods made it necessary to raise the road level on several occasions during the centuries.

On the right is a **sacellum** or votive chapel dedicated to an unknown divinity. Of particular interest is the polychrome mosaic pavement dating to the middle of the 2nd century A.D. (although some experts place it in a later period): it is one of the oldest polychrome mosaics from the Imperial age, created during a time when the use of black and white tessarae still prevailed.

At a short distance ahead, on the right, are the remains of the **Portico of the Sloping Roof** or Portico del Tetto Spiovente (first half of the 2nd century A.D.) running along the Decumanus for over 100 metres. Behind the portico is a row of shops with upper floors, followed by a complex of warehouses for foodstuffs (*horrea*). The latter, which can be dated to the end of the 2nd century A.D., were the largest in the city and have never been completely excavated. They

were divided into *cellae* with floors raised on small pillars to protect the grain from the damp. Their construction clearly shows how Ostia, even after the building of Trajan's port, was a focal point for the food trade for at least the second century of the Empire. Continuing to walk along the Decumanus in a westerly direction, you will notice another of the **Cippi of Caninius** (below the level of the road surface), followed by a section of the great lead **Fistula** (tube) through which most of the water was piped into the city as from the early Imperial age.

On the right, you can see the remains of the **Portico of Neptune**, originally 155 metres long, and formed of thirty porticoes with brick pillars and travertine plinths and capitals, possibly surmounted by further orders of porticoes. Dating

to the period of Hadrian, it was intended to monumentalise this side of the street, overlooked by some of the city's main buildings.

Worth noting among the latter are the **Baths of Neptune** or Terme di Nettuno (Fig. 2). Steps lead from the Decumanus to a terrace providing a bird's-eye view of the entire bath complex: on the left, the gymnasium surrounded on three sides by a colonnade and with a huge cistern underneath, built before the baths (you enter from the north-east corner); on the right, various rooms which will be described below. The entrance halls (Rooms 1 and 2) with figurative mosaics: the first depicts Amphitrite riding a seahorse accompanied by Tritons; in the centre of the second one, which is undoubtedly one of Ostia's finest mosaics, is Neptune driving seahorses

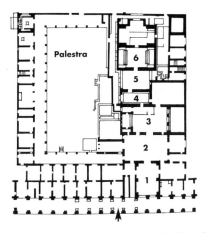

Fig. 2. Baths of Neptune.
1. Vestibule (mosaic depicting Amphitrite); 2 Vestibule (mosaic depicting Neptune); 3 *frigidarium*; **4 and 5** *tepidaria*; **6** *caldarium*.

**Baths of Neptune,
gymnasium** (left).
**Baths of Neptune, mosaic
with Neptune and marine
retine** (above).

and surrounded by fantastic animals and figures from the sea world. In the north, you can make out the *frigidarium* (Room 3) with two pools (the right one is set off by two columns) whose floor is decorated with a mosaic depicting Scylla surrounded by other sea monsters. This is followed by two *tepidaria* (Rooms 4 and 5) heated by warm air circulating under the floor and in the walls through small terracotta tubes; then there is a *caldarium* (Room 6) with two pools for hot baths, and,

finally, a second *caldarium*, which later fell out of use. Running alongside the eastern wall of the heated rooms is a service corridor through which the heat supplied by the furnaces was distributed. In this sector, at the north-east corner, is a cistern located at a higher level, which was filled by a water pipe supported by travertine brackets. The baths, which were built under Domitian, are linked to the names of Emperors Hadrian and Antoninius Pius who provided for their reconstruction (139 A.D.)

and decoration; further restoration was carried out at the end of the 2nd century A.D., by Lucilius Gamala *iunior*, a descendant of one of the most ancient and prominent families of Ostia, and during the 4th century A.D.

The restoration carried out under Lucilius Gamala possibly involved the reinforcement of the eastern wall of the *caldaria* and in the closure of the last great *caldarium*. Walking along Via dei Vigili you can see the outer side of the eastern wall of the building leading to the heated rooms described above.

Below street level, on the right, you can see another curious **mosaic** depicting male heads, the personifications of a number of Roman provinces (Africa covered with elephant skin; Egypt with a crocodile, Sicily with three legs, Spain crowned with olive leaves) and others symbolising the winds (and in a broader sense, navigation). The mosaic, which belongs to a previously existing bath building subsequently covered by the road and other constructions may

Mosaic of the Provinces, Egypt.

have been intended as the symbolic commemoration (through its allusions to sea trade by means of the aforementioned provinces) of the construction of the port under Emperor Claudius, thanks to which Ostia was to become the hub of sea trade.

Going back, you follow the Portico of Neptune as far as Via della Fontana where the **Caupona of Fortunatus** is located: the building in question was an inn selling beverages as can be deduced from the presence of a mosaic pavement inscription from the beginning of the 3rd century A.D.: *(dicit) Fortunatus vinum e cratera quod sitis bibe* ["Fortunatus says: if you're thirsty, drink from the large bowl"].

Turn right along the evocative Via della Fontana which takes its name from the **fountain** set on the right side, one of the best preserved in Ostia, with a barrel vault, two taps and a drainage channel for the water pouring over the edge. Along the left side of the road is a long narrow block (originally three or four floors high) with shops and apartments divided into three sections by two corridors: these passageways joined Via della Fontana with Via delle Corporazioni which was overlooked by the double facade of the residential complex.

The three sections of the block are conventionally known as the Insula of the Child Hercules, the Insula of the Painted Ceiling, and the Block of the Furnaces. You can visit the central section of the block, occupied by the **Insula of the Painted Ceiling** (Insula del Soffitto Dipinto), by going through the central covered passageway. This is a classic example of an exclusive residence well documented in Ostia, suited to the needs of wealthy middle class. The house consists of a corridor running along the front and receiving light from windows looking onto the street (Via della Fontana), off which three rooms and a drawing-room (by the entrance hall) open.

The first room on the right after the entrance contains frescoes decorating the walls with red and yellow panels separated by two Ionic columns, in the typical style of the late Antonine age (end of the 2nd century A.D.); also of interest are the ceiling paintings (giving the *insula* its name) divided into diamonds and squares; these too are characteristic of the period.

You now go back to the Via della Fontana and turn off into Via della Palestra. On the left is the entrance to the **Firemen's Barracks** (Caserma dei Vigili). This building housed the fire-brigade whose task it was to put out the frequent fires that often not only damaged homes but, more importantly, the granaries which were of fundamental importance not only to Ostia, but to Rome itself. Claudius was the first to assign an urban cohort with fire-fighting responsibilities to the city, but it was not until the end of the 1st century A.D., that a specialised permanent secondment was stationed there, under the authority of a tribune and formed of 400 *vigiles* under the command of four centurions. The barracks were built around A.D. 90, as shown by excavations, but the building's current layout dates to the complete renovation carried out under Hadrian (A.D. 130); extensive restoration was

Firemen's Barracks.

carried out at the beginning of the 3rd century A.D. One could enter the barracks through three wide doors flanked by pilasters: the main entrance was on Via dei Vigili, and the two side entrances opened onto Via della Palestra and Via della Fullonica, respectively. The complex, which was originally two-storeyed if not higher, consists of a porticoed courtyard onto which the rooms open. On the rear side is the *Augusteum*, a room dedicated to the Imperial cult with a floor mosaic depicting the sacrifice of a bull.

In this room and in the courtyard are numerous plinths bearing inscriptions with dedications to various emperors (from Antoninius Pius to Gordian), some of

Christian Oratory, sarcophagus with depiction of Orpheus (detail).

which mention the fire-brigade. Two drinking troughs stand in the corners of the courtyard. Of particular interest is the latrine to the left of the main entrance with the typical marble seats. There is also an aedicule dedicated to Fortuna Sancta, a divinity often venerated in public latrines according to a tradition heavily criticised in Christian circles (see the works of the ecclesiastic writer Titus Flavius

Clementes, who lived between the second half of the 2nd and the beginning of the 3rd centuries A.D.).

Outside the main entrance on Via dei Vigili are two mosaics showing craters or large drinking receptacles, probably relating to the two wine shops reserved for the military.

You now go back onto the Decumanus and walk as far as the **Christian Oratory**, one of the few Christian buildings known in Ostia: it was built near to the site where, in A.D. 269, many Christian martyrs from Ostia, including St. Aurea, were put to death near an arch in front of the theatre ("ad Arcum ante Teatrum" according to the *Liber Pontificalis*). The oratory consists of a room with an apse built during the early

Horrea of Hortensius.

Theatre, marble theatrical mask.

Middle Ages using masonry that recycled existing materials. On top of one wall is a sarcophagus depicting Orpheus playing the lyre (identified with Christ) with a typical Christian funerary inscription on one edge: *Hic Quiriacus dormit in pace* ["Here Quiriacus rests in peace"]: it has been suggested that the deceased is the homonymous bishop of Ostia, but identification is not certain. The oratory was a place of worship until the Middle Ages (documented by written evidence from 1162) when it was the destination for processions which left Gregoriopolis to travel along the Decumanus between buildings that were by then in ruins and partially buried.

On the left of the Decumanus, at a level below that of the road, you can see the **Horrea of Hortensius,** dating to the Julian-Claudian period. These are the colony's oldest warehouses and may have

been built following the trade expansion boosted by the construction of Claudius' port. The complex has a rectangular courtyard surrounded by tufa pillars with corner columns made of travertine, and *cellae* with walls in *opus reticulatum*. The building underwent subsequent renovations and modifications, clearly evident in the masonry of the rooms on the west side, which were restored during the Severan age. In the second half of the 3rd century A.D., a *sacellum* was built to the right of the entrance, with a mosaic pavement depicting a disc with rays (possibly the Sun God) and bearing the following inscription: *Horte(n)sius Heraclida n(avarcus) cl(assis) pr(aetoriae) Mis(enensis) / ex voto templum fecit Iulius Victorinus sacerdos tessallavit* ["Lucius Hortensius Heraclida, commander of the Praetorian fleet of Misenum

built this temple. The priest Julius Victorinus had the mosaic carried out"].

You now return to the Decumanus by the main entrance to the theatre. Here you can see the remains of three brick pillars (originally four) forming an **Honorary Arch** built in A.D. 216 in honour of Emperor Caracalla; part of the architectural decorations are now set on top of these pillars. As mentioned earlier, in A.D. 269, this site provided the backdrop to the martyrdom of St. Aurea and other Christians (*ad Arcum ante teatrum*).

The **Theatre**, which is one of the oldest existing brick theatres, was built during the Augustan age, between the first and second Consulate of Agrippa (as the inscription informs us), the emperor's son-in-law who died in 12 B.C. Large sections of wall in *opus reticulatum* together with the remains of the tufa pillars supporting the 17

THEATRICAL ENTERTAINMENT
It is hard to establish with any precision what plays were staged in Roman theatres. It is probable that between the end of the 1st century B.C. and the early Imperial age the tragedies of Ennius, Accius and Pacuvius, and the comedies of Plautus and Terence were staged. But the wider public preferred the more popular, undemanding shows of *Atellan*, mime and pantomime. *Atellan* (from Atella, a town in Campania) was a farce with stock characters (Maccus, the stupid glutton, Pappus, the old fool, Dossenus, the shrewd hunchback, etc). During the 1st century B.C., mime, which was based on the gestures and dancing of the actors, still possessed some literary qualities, but it rapidly degenerated into obscene comedy. Pantomime was a show with dance and music whose subject was often mythological but also based on episodes from everyday life, with a certain erotic or orgiastic licence.

Theatre.

arches of the portico behind the stage belong to this first phase. Nevertheless, during the late Imperial age (end of the 2nd century A.D.), the building, whose capacity was no longer adequate to the needs of a constantly growing population, was radically remodelled and extended to hold an audience of 3,500-4,000 persons. This remodelled version of the theatre is the one surviving today.

Outside is a brick portico originally two orders high (a section near the entrance has been completely reconstructed) housing a row of shops, while four steep steps lead directly into the middle section of the seating area (cavea).

The main entrance consists of a central corridor with barrel-vault leading to the *orchestra*: unique to the Ostian theatre, this feature has never been encountered in any of the known ancient theatres. From the semi-circular space of the orchestra (now grassed over but originally paved with

marble slabs) you can admire the spacious seating area; extensively rebuilt, it originally had three tiers of seats of which only the first two have survived. The three rows of marble steps near the orchestra were places of honour reserved for notables. In the lower section of the seating area are the remains of a marble parapet which separated it from the orchestra steps when the latter, in accordance with a popular tradition of the late Imperial age, was flooded for aquatic games; water was piped through the central passageway from two cisterns formed by the shops under the theatre portico.

The lower part of the proscenium holds a number of curved and rectangular niches; three marble masks and some architectural elements that decorated the *frons scenae* are displayed on a tufa wall at the rear.

Behind the proscenium are several cipolin pillars erroneously placed on top of the remains of the tufa

pillars forming the external portico, originally set on the loggia above the last row of steps (*summa cavea*).

The orchestra could also be reached via two side passages (*paradoi*) whose walls are still covered by extensive sections of the *opus reticulatum* facing dating to the earlier phase. Set into the wall of the eastern parados is the inscription commemorating the restructuring of the theatre by Septimius Severus and his son Caracalla, referred to as Caesar, therefore not yet elected to rule the empire (A.D. 196-197).

Behind the theatre is a truly singular complex, one that has not been encountered in any other of the Roman cities known to us: the **Square of the Guilds** or (Piazzale delle Corporazioni, see Fig. 3): a huge open area, surrounded by a colonnade on three sides. Originally designed as the *porticus post scenam* of the adjacent theatre in order to provide shelter or an area where you could go for a stroll, it subsequently became a focal point for the commercial activities being carried out between Ostia (and therefore Rome) and the Mediterranean provinces.

Built during the Augustan age with walls in *opus reticulatum*, during the first phase of its existence the Forum consisted of a covered passageway running around three sides of the central area, forming an integral part of the theatre complex. During the Claudian period, the floor level was raised and the first real portico was built with a single row of brick pillars. Under Hadrian, the floor was raised further, to the current level, and a second row of columns was added, creating a double colonnade.

From middle of the 2nd century A.D. to the Severan age, if not longer, the complex was gradually decorated with mosaics with depictions and inscriptions referring to Mediterranean commerce and to the various categories of trade of the individual guilds. During the 3rd century A.D., partitions divided the internal space into small rooms (stationes) which were the commercial offices of the entrepreneurs and merchants who wished to publicise their activities, which were also clearly depicted in the mosaic pavements. Below are the descriptions of some of the mosaics and inscriptions that decorated the 61 *stationes* of the forum:

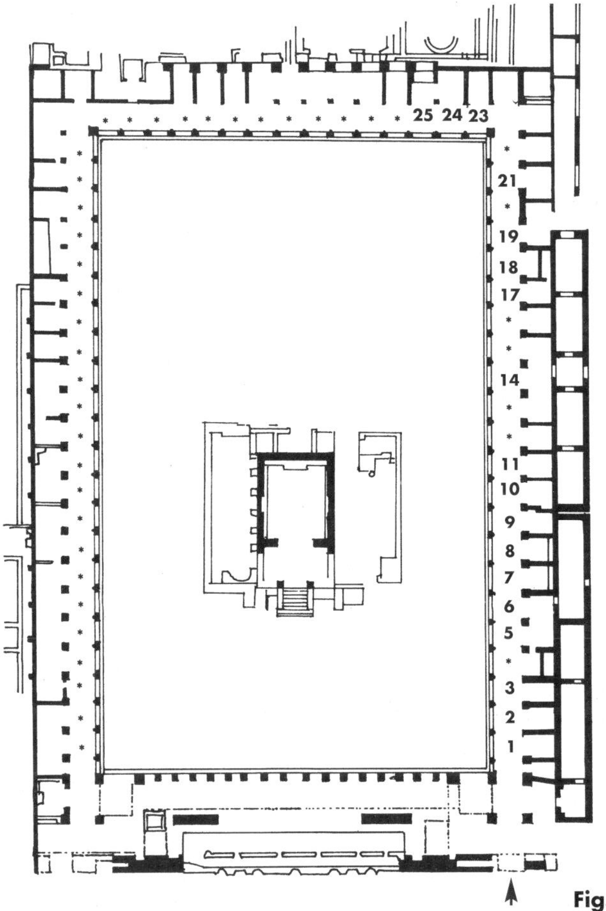

Fig. 3.
Square of the Guilds.

No. 1 Ansate plaque with the following inscription: *[Cl]odius Primigenius [Cl]audius Crescens q(uin)q(uennales) stuppatores res(tiones)* ["Clodius Primigenius and Claudius Crescens, heads of the tow and rope traders guild"].

No. 2 Ansate plaque with the following inscription: *Corpus pellion(um) Ost(iensium) et Porte(nsium) hic* ["The guild of tanners from Ostia and Portus (is) here"].

No. 3 Two ships, one on each side of the lighthouse of Ostia. Inscription: *Navicularium lignariorum* ["of shipowners who transport and sell timber"]. Timber was an extremely important material and used both for shipbuilding as well as for other purposes like heating the baths. For this reason, during the later Imperial period, shipowners trading in timber enjoyed special privileges by order of the State.

No. 5 *Statio* with a depiction of a *mensor* (wheat measurer) using a *rutellum* (scraper) to smooth the grain in a *modius* or corn-measure, a container used as the official unit of measure (around 7 kg). Grain imports obviously represented the most important aspect of Ostian trade activities.

No. 6-9 Depictions of *modius* and *dolphins*.

No. 10 Depiction of two fish, one to either side of a *modius*. Inscription: *navicularii Misuenses hic* ["the guild of shipowners

Square of the Guilds, mosaic from the *statio* of the *navicularii Karalitani*.

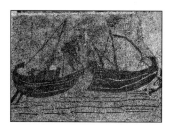

Square of the Guilds, mosaic with scene of amphorae being unloaded.

from Misua is here"]. *Misua* was a city in proconsular Africa, near Carthage.

No. 11 Depiction of Cupid riding a dolphin and two medallions with female heads, maybe personifications of the seasons. Inscription: *navicularii Mu(s)lu(vit)a(ni) ? hic* ["the guild of shipowners from *Musluvium* is here"]. If the reading is correct, the place in question is *Musluvium*, another African city in *Mauretania Sifitensis*, in what is now western Morocco.

No. 14 Depiction of an elephant. Inscription: *Stat(io) Sabratensium* ["Office of the Sabratans"]. Sabrata was a Tripolitan city belonging to the province of proconsular Africa (now Libya). The elephant symbolised the ivory trade, but the animal itself was often used in circus games and parades.

No. 17 Inscription: *Naviculari Gummitani* ["shipowners from Gumma"]. Gumma was a city in proconsular Africa, not far from Carthage.

No. 18 Inscription: *navicul(arii) Karthag(inienses) de suo*

["the shipowners from Carthage at their expense"]. During the Imperial age, Carthage was one of the leading commercial centres in the Mediterranean.

No. 19 Inscription: *Navic(ularii) Turritani* ["the shipowners from Turris"]. Many ancient cities were called Turris, but in this case the town involved may be *Turris or Turres Libisonis*, corresponding to the modern Porto Torres in Sardinia.

No. 21 Depiction of a ship between two *modii*. Inscription: *navic(ularii) et negontiantes Karalitani* ["shipowners and merchants from *Karales*"]. *Karales* corresponds to present-day Cagliari in Sardinia.

No. 23 Above, depictions of the lighthouse and two ships; below, two dolphins and a crab. Inscription: *(navic)ulari Syllect(ni)* ["shipowners from *Syllectum*"]. The incorrectly restored tessarae make the inscription hard to read. *Syllectum* was a city in Byzacium (now Tunisia) in the province of proconsular Africa.

No. 24 Scene depicting a porter unloading an amphora from a cargo ship onto a river boat (*navis caudicaria*).

No. 25 Depiction of a river, the Nile (or maybe the Rhone), with three-mouthed delta and a ship-bridge.

The actual square, which may also have been covered by grass in ancient times, is decorated with statues of well-deserving citizens (often described in the

inscriptions as guild members) while the centre is occupied by a **temple** from the end of the 1st century A.D., with a high podium and two-columned pronaos. Although thought in the past to have been dedicated to Ceres, the goddess of the harvests and of abundance (and in a wider sense, of the prosperity resulting from commerce), there is no hard evidence for this theory.

In the last room on the western side of the portico is the copy (the original is in the Museo Nazionale Romano) of the altar with depictions of episodes of the origins of Rome, including Faustolus and the twins with the she-wolf.

By the south-west corner of the square is the so-called **Domus of Apuleius**, one of the few examples of Ostian housing during the transitional phase between the early and middle Imperial age. Built during Trajan's reign, the building underwent remodelling around the middle of the 2nd century A.D., and at the beginning of the 3rd century A.D. In the past, the owner was thought to have been a member of the important

Sacred Area of Four Small Temples.

Gamala family. Although there is no concrete evidence for this hypothesis, a lead pipe bearing the name *P. Apuleius* was found on the site and may indicate the owner of the domus, at least during a certain period. The house's unusual floor plan was determined by lack of space. A narrow vestibule leads to an eight-pillared atrium with an impluvium, a layout typical of the 1st century domus, although the porticoed courtyard anticipates the building style used in Ostian houses of the middle Empire. On the left is the second wing formed by a corridor behind which are two rows of rooms, some decorated with outstanding mosaics. The *tablinum* contains one such mosaic with a design of concentric circles and triangles converging in the centre, where there is a depiction of the head of the Gorgon (middle of 2nd century A.D.).

At a short distance ahead, on the right, is the **Mithraeum of the Seven Spheres** (Mitreo delle Sette Sfere), dedicated to the god Mithras. The cult, which was Persian in origin, was introduced to Rome and Italy during the second half of the 2nd century A.D. by legionaries returning from the East. Like all mithraeums, there is a podium or bench on either side where the faithful sat to eat their sacred meals during the religious ceremonies. At the back is a cast of a relief (the original is in the Vatican Museums) depicting Mithras wearing a short tunic and in the act of slaying a bull, the symbol of the victory of light over darkness. The floor is decorated with a mosaic depicting the seven planets (moon, Mercury, Jupiter, Mars, Venus and Saturn) representing the seven phases of initiation through which the faithful had to pass. Echoing this symbolism are the signs of the zodiac on the tops of the benches.

South of the Mithraeum is the Sacred Area of the **Four Small Temples** (Area Sacra dei Quattro Tempietti), one of the colony's oldest sanctuaries. The main monument in the complex is formed by four small temples of the same size built on top of a single high 34-metre-long podium with walls in *opus quasi-reticulatum*. The first sacellum on the left has a mosaic pavement with an inscription containing the name of the Duovir (or leading magistrate) C. Cartilius Poplicola, Ostia's most prominent public figure towards the end of the 1st century B.C. In the pronaos of the last temple on the right is an altar with a dedication reading *Veneri sacrum* ["consecrated to Venus"]. This inscription and the characteristics of the masonry allow us to link the complex to another epigraph from the first half of the 1st century B.C. mentioning four temples dedicated to Venus, Fortuna, Hope, and Ceres built by P. Lucilius Gamala, who belonged to one of Ostia's most prominent families. It should be mentioned that at the time of construction (presumably 90-60 B.C.), the sanctuary was in an extra-urban area, outside the *castrum walls*, and close to the river port. Its dedication to four divinities of good omen, to whom all those involved in shipping and trade were particularly devoted, was obviously linked to its location.

Looming up on the right of the Decumanus, you will see the **Collegiate Temple** (Tempio Collegiale), built at the end of the 2nd century A.D. by the builders' guild (*fabri tignuarii*), possibly Ostia's most powerful professional association. Identification was made possible by the discovery of an inscription on the architrave, now set onto a wall facing the Decumanus, with a text containing a dedication to the deified Emperor Pertinax (*Divo Pertinaci*, therefore dating to A.D. 193) made by the guild in question.

We now return to the Decumanus and walk along it for a short stretch, then turn right into a minor *cardo* which will take us to the **Great Horrea** (Grandi Horrea, see Fig. 4), one of the city's largest storage facilities. Built halfway through the 1st century A.D., after the opening of Claudius' port, in response to the intensification of the city's commercial activities, the warehouses were restructured and extended at the end of the 2nd century A.D. and during the Severan age.

The main entrance was in the north side, facing the Tiber, but there were also secondary entrances in the western and eastern sides of the complex.
The *Horrea* consists of 64

cellae, the oldest of which were built along the east, west and south outer walls around a courtyard with a tufa-pillared portico in its centre. During the age of Commodus, two parallel rows of cellae were built in the space bordered by the portico along a common rear wall, in accordance with a layout mainly documented at Portus. The cellae were also equipped with *suspensurae*, or small pillars supporting a raised floor. The presence of *suspensurae* which were used to protect stored goods from the damp, indicates that these warehouses were used for grain.

Finally, the entire northern wing, containing even larger rooms, was built ex-novo during the Severan period. During its first phase (1st century A.D.) the complex had outer walls built of large tufa blocks in *opus quadratum*: this technique, no longer used in the Imperial age, was used in the *horrea* to withstand the strong sideways thrust of the weight of the grain, as well as to protect this precious foodstuff from fire. The extensions and

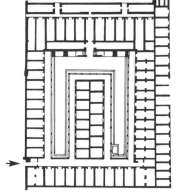

Fig. 4. Great Horrea.

restorations undergone by the Great Horrea between the end of the 2nd and the beginning of the 3rd centuries A.D. clearly show that even after the construction of Trajan's port, Ostia did not suffer any form of economic decline. On the contrary, it had to increase its storage structures to respond to the growth in commercial activities.

We now return to the Decumanus and walk along it to the cross-roads with Via dei Molini. On the corner is a **Republican Temple** with a podium in *opus quasi-reticulatum* and moulded cornices from the first half of the 1st century B.C. The identity of the divinity to whom it is dedicated remains unknown.

from the
CASTRUM
to the FORUM

Turning right into Via dei Molini, to your left you will see the best preserved section of the Republican **Castrum** walls. Built with tufa stone blocks set in rows of headers and stretchers in the *opus quadratum* technique, the walls formed a rectangular fortress 194 metres by 125 metres. The two main roads, Decumanus and Cardo, ran through the fortified citadel, crossing in the centre and dividing it into four equal areas. Four gates were set into the walls at the entry and exit points of the roads. Other tufa walls in *opus quadratum* were built onto the outside of the fortress walls, probably the boundary walls of *tabernae*, or shops, and certainly dating to a later period (maybe the second half of the 3rd century B.C.) when the fortress no longer had any defensive purpose. Set into this side of the castrum is the western gate which you can see when you go back onto the Decumanus: the level of this stretch of road is lower than that of the Imperial age and corresponds to the Republican age.

The gate, which has only one fornix, or arch, contains two spaces and was originally tower-shaped.

Returning to Via dei Molini, to your left you will see the **Mill Building** (Edificio dei Molini) built in *opus mixtum*, around A.D. 120. Paved rooms hold several lava millstones which were used to grind the grain. The machinery consisted of a conical lower structure (*meta*) with a moving section on top (*catillus*) that was turned by means of a bar pushed by slaves or mules, blindfolded to stop them becoming dizzy. The grains fell through a funnel-shaped container hanging from the ceiling into the machinery where they were crushed to powder by the friction between the stones. The rooms in the north side hold cylindrical containers with two holes (made of lava stone) for making dough known as *machinae quibus farinae subiguntur* ["machinery used to handle the flour"]. Another room contains two ovens for bread-baking. In fact, the activities linked to all three phases of bread-baking were carried out here: milling, kneading of the dough and baking.

According to literary, legal and epigraphic evidence the trade of the miller/baker (*pistor*) was very widespread and those engaged in it belonged to a very important guild, that of the *pistores*. In fact, bread from Ostia (called *pane ostiensis*) was even transported to Rome where it may have been distributed free to the people or sold at a subsidised price: this explains why the Ostian *pistores*, at the beginning of

Mill Building.

27

House of Diana.

luxury home developing horizontally and often covering large areas, facing inwards onto the open spaces of the atrium and gardens.

Ostia's *insulae* (built at least fifty years after the last Pompeian houses) provided housing for the people and occupied an extremely restricted horizontal space (300-400 sq. m.), while extending upwards, reaching up to four or five floors in height. The apartments received light from an inner courtyard and from the windowed balconies facing the outside.

A clay tablet depicting Diana and located inside the courtyard gave the house, one of the most famous in Ostia, its name. Recent studies have modified previous knowledge about this complex as well as the presumed layout of the rooms, uncovering the various floor levels relating to the different construction phases.

The north part of the house contains an attractive polychrome geometric mosaic with rosettes and plaited elements decorating the original side corridor. In the rear is a huge *triclinium*, or dining room, with floors containing coloured marble inlays (*opus sectile*). The floors date to the reign of Hadrian (1st phase) when the house was already a luxurious complex with a porticoed courtyard onto which the rooms, including the *triclinium*, opened. The addition of a nymphaeum in

the 3rd century A.D., claimed the same rights as the Roman bakers.

Entering the nearby Via di Diana, on your right you will see the **House of Diana** (Casa di Diana) which dates to the reign of Hadrian and is an interesting example of the most widespread type of Ostian housing: the *insulae*, large multi-storied tenement blocks built around a porticoed courtyard. This high-density housing became necessary from the beginning of the 2rd century A.D. onwards, when the boost to social and economic life provided by the construction of Trajan's port had a knock-on effect on population. The old Pompeian-type *domus* (1st century B.C. - 1st century A.D.) was a high-class

PRIVATE CONSTRUCTION

During the course of the 2nd century A.D., private construction was characterised by the rise of new models of housing answering the needs of the different social classes that had become stratified during the middle Empire: a) the popular *insula*, or multi-storey tenement block often with a central porticoed courtyard and *tabernae* on the ground floor; b) the high-class *insula* with large inner porticoed courtyard; c) the modest but respectable house corresponding to the needs of the lower middle-class, formed of a main corridor running along the facade off which all the rooms opened; d) the house formed by a long central corridor off which all the rooms opened; e) an original type of high-class residential complex, formed by regular blocks of apartments surrounded by a large garden area.

the centre of the courtyard and the decoration of the ambulatory with a geometric olive-leaf-patterned mosaic pavement date to halfway through the 2nd century A.D. (2nd phase). In the north-west corner you can see other mosaics, some from the Hadrianic period, some more recent, from middle of the 3rd century A.D. (3rd phase) with irregular geometric patterns. The rear section of this wing holds a mithraeum built during a later period on top of the previous 2nd and 3rd-century structures. The mithraeum consists of an aedicule in front of which is an altar with a circular cavity. Only the low front walls of the side podia – which covered the more recent mosaic pavements dating to the 3rd phase – survive.

In the south section of the building is a rectangular room with painted walls containing slender architectural motifs and other designs on a white background, dating to the Antonine age (A.D. 160-170). During a later period (4th-5th century A.D.) the room was transformed into a stable and roughly repaved. The current floor level (of which sections in opus spicatum still survive) throughout the house dates to late Antiquity (from the 4th century A.D. onwards), when the floor was raised and a fountain was built in the courtyard, covering the older nymphaeum. An outside staircase near the entrance led to the upper floor which has a similar layout; a number of steps on the third floor still survive.

Opening onto the facade was a row of ground-floor shops with inside staircases leading to the shop-owner's living-quarters, a mezzanine with a small window. A continuous balcony, formed of a series of small vaults, originally with a parapet, ran along the building front above the shops. The House of Diana originally had four or five floors, reaching a total height of 18-20 m, the maximum permitted by building regulations.

Further ahead, on the left, is one of the most evocative buildings of Ostia, the **Insula of the Thermopolium** (Caseggiato del Termopolium), dating to the Hadrianic age, inserted into the urban fabric by means of a practical and original solution: from the entrance in Via di Diana, a vaulted passageway leads to a courtyard lined with *tabernae* linking up with the Decumanus on the other side. The facade overlooking Via di Diana has a balcony with depressed arches resting on travertine brackets, an architectural feature that would be used in the Middle Ages. Below are the three entrances to an inn, commonly known as *thermopolium* (but more correctly defined as *popina*), which was opened here in the 3rd century, replacing the existing taverns.

The inn, which faces the street, consists of three rooms, of which the middle one is the main room. It has a large counter with three display shelves for the food

Thermopolium, exterior.

Thermopolium, interior.

and drink on sale and a small sink where the dishes were washed. A plaque with an inscription dedicated to Fulvius Plazianus, the praetorian prefect killed by Caracalla in A.D. 205 was used to make the sink allowing us to date the construction of the *thermopolium* to the 3rd century A.D.

Running along an inner wall is a second counter also with display shelves above which hangs a painting depicting the food usually offered in the inn: eggs, olives, fruit, and hot radishes served as an antipasto. On the right is the kitchen with a *dolium* (huge terracotta jar) fitted into the floor, used to keep wine and water cool, and the fire. The room on the left has a floor decorated with a mosaic originating from the upper floor from which it was removed after excavation. Its purpose is unknown. The rear part of the premises is occupied by a small courtyard with a fountain and stone seats.

On the opposite side of the street is the **Insula of the Paintings** (Caseggiato dei Dipinti), from the time of Hadrian, which, like the House of Diana, is distinguished by the considerable height of the building. This insula is characterised by its unusual layout composed of three separate blocks set out in an

L-shape, overlooking Via di Diana and Via dei Dipinti, around the fulcrum of a common courtyard. A steep staircase goes from Via di Diana to the second floor from which the visitor can enjoy a panoramic view of the excavations. Of the three *insulae* - known as the Insulae of the Paintings, of the Young Bacchus, and of Jupiter and Ganymede - the latter is the most interesting to visit.

The house consists of a central corridor, a small courtyard (originally linked to the larger common courtyard) and painted rooms. The *tablinum* which had a window opening onto the small courtyard is famous for the wall frescoes with a central panel depicting Jupiter and Ganymede in a blend of coloured panels and slender architectural motifs. To the right of the corridor is a room with frescoes typical of the so-called 'yellow rooms' characterised by a yellow background with slender architectural motifs and other decorative motifs (birds, garlands, etc.). The paintings date to the end of the 2nd century A.D., when the use of architectural designs, a style that became popular during the early Imperial age, had already waned.

Returning, we enter the **Forum** (Fig. 5). The political and civil centre of Roman cities, the Forum was often a large rectangular open space surrounded by religious and public

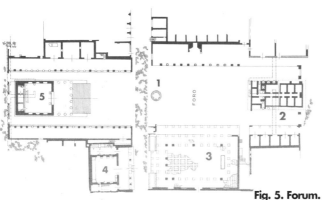

Fig. 5. Forum.
1 Sacellum of Lares Augusti;
1 Temple of Roma and Augustus; 3 Basilica;
2 "Curia"; 5 Capitolium.

Capitolium.

buildings. The area in question was used from the Republican age onwards, but it was not until the Imperial period that it became the Forum, taking on its current monumental appearance.

The main sacred building is the **Capitolium**. Dedicated to Jupiter, Juno and Minerva, the capitolium was present in all Roman colonies because it was considered to be the transposition of the main State cult, that is the Capitoline Triad – Jupiter, Juno and Minerva – to whom Rome's Capitoline temple was dedicated. The Ostian building dates to around A.D. 120 with a high podium and staircase in the front, completely made out of bricks. There were six columns in the front and another two by the sides of the pronaos. There is a podium for the three statues of the cult at the rear of the cella and niches are set into its walls. The entrance threshold is made from a single, extremely precious block of African marble.

If you look at the temple from a certain distance away, it is possible to distinguish the relieving arches along the masonry which provided structural strength by ensuring the equal distribution of the weight of the long walls.

Only the bare brick skeleton of the temple remains; the precious marbles that originally faced the walls were removed from the Middle Ages onwards. Facing the stairs is the altar. From this area it is possible to see the previous Republican-period buildings at a lower level and the tufa foundations of the Capitolium from the end of the 1st century B.C., next to the original Cardo Maximus: these buildings were apparently knocked down in the Imperial age when the square was remodelled according to the new criteria of town-planning (e.g. the Cardo was cancelled) in a more monumental, spectacular style.

Alongside the Decumanus is the **Sacellum of the Lares Augusti**, a round

brick building with marble foundations. The facing slabs, some with inscriptions, allowed the temple to be identified. According to epigraphic evidence the sacellum dates to the middle of the 1st century A.D. and was dedicated to the cult of the Lares, the household gods usually protecting the family, but in this particular case, protecting the imperial family.

On the opposite side of the square stands the **Temple of Roma and Augustus**, built at the beginning of the 1st century A.D. and also identified with the help of an epigraphic document. All that is left of the building are the parts in *opus reticulatum*; nevertheless, the fragments of the rear pediment have been reassembled and set, together with a statue of the goddess of Victory, on a purpose-built wall along the east side. Another simulacrum, found in situ, represents the goddess Roma dressed as an Amazon with one foot resting on the globe, symbolising Roman domination of the world: the statue is now set at the back of the temple where it probably originally stood. The layout of the forum, with its two main buildings, the temple of Roma and Augustus and the Capitolium (facing each other on either side of the square) assumes a precise ideological meaning: it symbolised the power of Rome represented by the figure of the emperor whose importance was equal to that of the Capitoline Triad.

Standing on the eastern side of the Forum is the **Basilica**, built between the end of the 1st century A.D. and the beginning of the 2nd century A.D., where legal activities and commercial operations were carried out. The building has a central nave and two side aisles; the nave is very wide and decorated with precious marbles of which only fragments survive. At the rear of the hall is the tribunal, or raised platform where the judge sat. The Basilica overlooked the Forum with a double portico with brick pillars faced with marble and decorated with a frieze of putti and festoons.

Next to the Basilica is the so-called **Round Temple** (Tempio Rotondo) whose precise purpose is unknown. It was built around the middle of the 3rd century A.D. and underwent major restoration under Constantine. It consists of a quadriportico, decorated with niches and columns, a stair leading to a ten-columned pronaos and, lastly, a circular cella with rectangular and semi-circular niches, originally covered by a dome. Near the entrance to the cella is a spiral staircase leading to the roof. It is thought that the monument, which is rather solemn and imposing, was the seat of the Ostian Senate on particularly important occasions. However, it has also been suggested that it

was the temple dedicated to the cult of the emperors.

Facing the basilica, on the opposite side of the Decumanus, at an angle to the Forum is the so-called **Curia**. Entering the six-pillared front, you go into a wide pronaos leading to a square room similar to a cella, flanked by two corridors. The brick masonry allows us to date it to the beginning of the 2nd century A.D. It was long-thought to have been the meeting-place of the council of decurions which was either located in the forum or in the vicinity. However, the discovery of numerous fragments relative to lists of *seviri augustales*, the guild responsible for the imperial cult (usually formed of freedmen, who, denied a career in municipal politics, could thus satisfy their desire for social ascent) suggest that this was their place of worship.

From the east side of the building we can see, at a lower level with respect to the Forum, the podium of the **Western Republican Temple** or Tempio repubblicano occidentale (end of 1st century B.C.) which is formed of three rows of tufa blocks framed by moulded cornices on the top and bottom. These were also razed to the ground when the Forum was reconstructed. The Forum of Ostia, as was the custom, was decorated with statues of local and Roman public figures. Epigraphic evidence tells us that there was an

equestrian statue of Hermogenes and a bronze statue of Gamala of which no trace remains. However, you can still see the plinth of an equestrian statue with a long inscription mentioning a 4th-century Prefect of the Annona, *M(anius) Aquilius Ru(sticus)* and an extremely important cippus from the middle of the 4th century A.D. bearing the following text: *Traslatam ex sordendibus locis / ad ornatum fori et ad faciem / publicam curante P(ublio) Attio /Clementino v(iro) c(larissimo) praef(ecto) ann(onae)* ["(Statue) transported here from squalid location to decorate the forum and its public image by order of Publio Attio Clementino, highly esteemed Prefect of the Annona"]. The contents of the epigraph tells us that during the late Imperial age the forum still carried out its public functions and that some areas of the suburbs were unhealthy or even abandoned.

Leaving the Forum from the east side, we enter the Via della Forica which leads to the **Baths of the Forum** (Terme del Foro, see Fig. 6), undoubtedly Ostia's finest and largest *thermae*. Although the complex might seem to be a public enterprise, the building was actually financed, around A.D. 160, by Marcus Gavius Maximus, Praetorian Prefect of Antoninius Pius; it underwent restoration on several occasions during the 4th and 5th centuries A.D.

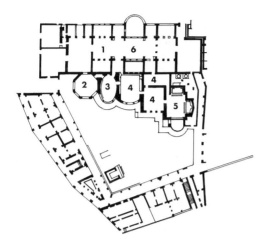

Fig. 6. Baths of the Forum.
1 *apodyterium;* **2** *heliocaminus;*
3 *laconicum;* **4** *tepidarium;*
5 *calidarium;* **6** *frigidarium.*

You enter the baths through a vestibule in the southern part of the complex, going along it from left to right. The rooms include the entrance hall (through which you still enter the baths today), an *apodyterium* consisting of two changing-rooms with two pillared entrances, a huge *frigidarium* with two pools (originally roofed by great cross vaults), another *apodyterium* similar to the previous one, and, finally, another vestibule. The south-facing rooms, which were heated as was the custom, have an unusual layout: their fronts are not lined up, but slightly staggered so as to ensure that they did not cover each other and could all receive the sun from the west during the afternoon when the *thermae* were usually at their most crowded. They were visited by passing through the same entrance hall that today's visitors use to enter the complex. The first octagonal room is a *heliocaminus* and was used for sun-bathing. The succession of rooms is as follows: an elliptical *laconicum* or sweating room; two *tepidaria*; a *calidarium* with three pools.

The numerous bone hairpins that came to light during the excavations prove that the baths were also visited by women, obviously during different hours, although this rule was not always respected.

South of the heated room is a trapezoidal gymnasium, surrounded by a portico with cipolin columns. On the south side of the portico is a hall with two rooms in the front and another room at the back with two spiral columns in the centre, possibly a 3rd-century guild-seat; on the south-western side is a small temple; behind it, a latrine followed by a row of *tabernae*.

Going back to the entrance of the baths, we exit onto Via della Forica. Opposite, on the right, is a **latrine**. It was built by transforming a workshop from the Hadrianic age, maybe at the time the *thermae* were being built, and was in use until well into the 4th century A.D. The latrine contains a row of twenty marble seats, each with its own hole, under which a channel ran for the waste water. You

Latrine.

Forum of the Heroic Statue.

enter the latrines through a revolving door whose central pivot hole can still be seen in the threshold stone.

Near the latrine, and behind the baths, is a huge square dating to the end of the 4th century A.D., surrounded by a colonnade, and known by the conventional name of **Forum of the Heroic Statue**. In the centre of the square stands a headless male statue in heroic nudity.

Going back down Via della Forica you return to the Forum where you see a plinth bearing an inscription with the following text: *Curavit / Ragonius Vincentius Celsus / praefectus annonae Urbis / et civitas fecit memorata de proprio* ["(The restoration ? of this complex) was carried out under Ragonius Vincentius Celsus, Prefect of the Annona of the

City of Rome.

The citizens of Ostia (have erected this statue) in his memory at their expense"]. The plinth probably held the statue of Ragonius Vincentius Celsus put up in his honour by the townsfolk of Ostia in recognition of his contribution, which may have been considerable, to the restoration of the Forum in the second half of the 4th century A.D.

from the FORUM to PORTA LAURENTINA

From the south side of the Forum, you take the Cardo Maximus. On your right, immediately after a nymphaeum, you will see the **Domus of Jupiter the Fulminator**. It owes its name to the fact that a cippus was found inside bearing this denomination in Greek (*Dii kataibatei*). The *domus*, built around the middle of the 2nd century B.C., still has the original late-Hellenistic layout despite the modifications carried out during the Imperial period.

The *fauces*, or entrance, flanked by two *tabernae*, leads to a Tuscan *atrium* with a marble impluvium in the centre. Columns made of large tufa blocks and side walls in opus incertum (the oldest parts of the building) originally defined the bedrooms (*cubicula*) which, as was the tradition, were situated alongside the atrium. In the rear was the reception chamber, the *tablinum*, which now appears as it did following restoration, with three niches (4th century A.D.).

Just a short distance ahead, on the right, is the Nymphaeum of the Eroti, which does not consist of

Nymphaeum of the Eroti.

the usual elegantly curved exedrae, but of a closed square space. Dating to the 4th century A.D., it is a single room with walls in brick and *opus vittatum* faced with precious marble slabs and with a basin (*labrum*) set in a square central pool. Set into the side walls are two niches holding copies of Eros stringing his bow, based on a famous sculpture by Lisippus (the originals are in the Museo Ostiense). The niche in the rear wall may have held a statue of Venus.

If you walk up the Cardo for a short stretch as far as the crossroads with Via della Caupona, on your right, you will find the **Domus of the Columns**, a typical home from late antiquity built with

an abundance of marbles and coloured mosaics. Built during the first half of the 3rd century A.D., it underwent restoration in two stages during the 4th century A.D. The vestibule leads to a central courtyard with a well and a nymphaeum with two apses; during the first half of the 4th century A.D. the portico was closed with partitions and the courtyard floor was raised and paved with marble slabs, while a mosaic made of large polychrome tesserae was added to the left side of the ambulatory and to the small exedra by the entrance. Opening off the rear of the courtyard, as in most domus, was the main living room, built during the later phase, with an entrance marked by

Domus of the Fish, courtyard.

two columns and a mosaic pavement with a central part in *opus sectile*. The chamber was heated as were the two small adjacent rooms on the south side.

Turning right off the Cardo Maximus, you enter Via della Caupona which takes you to the **Domus of the Fish** (Domus dei Pesci). This house from the late Imperial age (3rd century A.D.) was enlarged at the beginning of the 4th century by restructuring and transforming the masonry of an existing insula from the middle of the 2nd century A.D. The current entrance (which was originally secondary) leads to a central colonnaded courtyard with no less than three fountains dating to different periods. Opening off the southern side is the *tablinum*, set off by two columns, and featuring an outstanding mosaic pavement decorated with 48 panels containing various geometrical motifs. Facing the *tablinum* is a

sitting room with a floor in *opus sectile*.

A series of minor service rooms are located to the west of the ambulatory. The northern part of the house is the result of the 4th-century enlargement. The vestibule has a mosaic pavement with a design of a chalice holding a fish flanked by two further fish set in a polychrome *emblema*; behind the vestibule are three rooms,

one with a heating system. In the past, a number of experts maintained that the fish and chalice motif depicted in the mosaic in the entrance area (known symbols of the Christian faith) meant that the building belonged to some prominent Christian figure or even that it was the Ostian bishopric; theories that have now been discounted in the light of more recent studies and discoveries.

On the opposite side of the road is the **Caupona of the Peacock** (Caupona del Pavone), a private dwelling composed of one or two floors, built during the first decades of the 3rd century A.D. by modifying structures from the middle Imperial age. Around A.D. 250, it was transformed into an inn (*caupona*). A corridor leads to a small courtyard, in one corner of which there is a latrine. Leading off the left of another corridor, set

Caupona of the Peacock, room with bar.

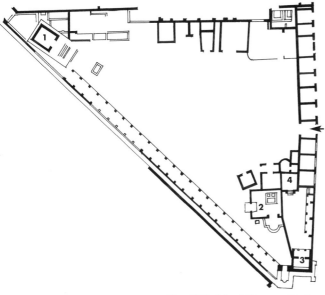

**Fig. 7 Field of Magna Mater.
1 Temple of Magna Mater; 2 Sacellum of Attis;
3 Temple of Bellona; 4 Schola of the Hastiferi.**

see Fig. 17). This vast triangular open space between the final stretch of the Cardo Maximus and the Republican Walls is a complex of temples, sacella and *scholae* dedicated to the cult of Magna Mater, the Oriental fertility goddess also known as Cybele. This cult was introduced to Rome in 204 B.C.

In his *Fasti* (IV 291f.) Ovid describes the arrival in Ostia of the ship transporting the black stone (symbol of the Phrygian goddess) from Pessinunte. The ship ran aground on a sandbank and was miraculously floated off by the Vestal Caludia Quinta who, after having been unjustly accused of having broken her vows of chastity, had called upon the goddess to provide some sign of her innocence. Although dating to the 1st century A.D., it was not nearly A.D. 150 that the complex took on its definitive appearance. As was customary for the religious buildings of oriental cults, the sanctuary was situated near the city-limits. The main entrance opens onto the Cardo Maximus which leads straight to the huge square where bulls were sacrificed in honour of the emperor (*taurobolia*). The main temple of Magna Mater was located in the western corner and originally had six pillared facade; only the podium in *opus reticulatum* with three arches on each side and the front staircase have survived.

orthoganally with respect to the entrance corridor, is a courtyard containing a household lararium with paintings depicting a peacock (unfortunately almost completely eroded by time) and, off the right, the main rooms. Most of the walls are decorated with frescoes dating to the Severan age (A.D. 210-220) distinguished by a system of prevalently red and yellow panels containing Dionysian figures and Muses, either standing or soaring in flight, with an abundant use of vegetal and animal decorations and less emphasis on the architectural divisions that distinguished painting during the early, and, to some extent, also the middle Imperial age. The main room is the *tablinum* which contains a bar with display shelves for food and sink for washing the dishes, added around the middle of the 3rd century A.D. The walls are decorated with red and yellow panels separated by columns and depicting male and female figures (the male figures may be philosophers); of particular interest a Genie suspended in the air, on the right of the entrance, and the fish below the sink in the counter. Set apart, on the left, is a small room covered with paintings of Dionysian subjects, skilfully depicted in impressionistic style and set out using the usual arrangement of coloured panels (without architectural divisions).

Walking back along the Cardo almost as far as Porta Laurentina we reach the **Field of Magna Mater** (Campo della Magna Mater,

RELIGIOUS LIFE: ORIENTAL CULTS

Ostia, a cosmopolitan centre and melting pot of people from different cultures and from often distant countries, was the home to a considerable number of oriental cults. Among these were the Cults of Isis and Serapis, whose diffusion was a by-product of commercial relations for the import of grain from Egypt, and whose popularity can be explained by the intrinsic characteristics of these divinities who were also considered the protectors of navigation and trade. There are numerous finds relating to the Phrygian cult of *Magna Mater* (or Cybele), the goddess of fertility, to whom the most imposing Ostian sanctuary was dedicated, even though relegated to the city-limits. It was widespread among the lower classes who perceived a symbolic allusion to life after death in the ceremonies of the rebirth of nature and spring. Another cult that enjoyed great success was Mithraism, a cult of Persian origin widely diffused during the 2nd and 3rd centuries A.D.: the divinity symbolises the victory of Good over Evil and the beneficial renewal of the world.

In the eastern sector, is the Sacellum of Attis, Cybele's shepherd lover who castrated himself in a fit of madness that was cast upon him by the goddess in punishment for his infidelty. The sacred area consists of a square courtyard with walls in *opus reticulatum* from the middle of the 1st century A.D., to which an apse with an entrance door flanked by two sculptures of Pan was added in the 3rd century A.D. Inside is a cast of a statue of Attis in a semi-reclining position (the original is in the Museo Profano Lateranense in Vaticano). Near the eastern corner is another small sacred complex formed by the Temple of Bellona (Italic goddess of war, associated with the cult of Magna Mater during the Imperial age) and the *scholae* of the lance-bearers (*hastiferi*) who carried out dances during the processions in honour of the goddess. Dating to the period around the middle of the 2nd century A.D., the Temple of Bellona, mainly built in *opus latericium*, has a pronaos with two columns, rectangular *cella* and rear podium.

On the opposite side of the sacred area is the Schola of the Hastiferi, consisting of a single *cella* with entrance stairs flanked by two columns and an interior embellished with marble decorations. A long brick colonnade runs along the Republican wall forming the southern boundary of the field. It is generally thought that the tower of the Imperial-age wall was used as a "fossa sanguinis", the cavity into which the initiate would be lowered to be bathed in the bull's blood running down through the holes of a wooden platform above; a ceremony which transmitted the bull's power to the faithful. It is, however, more likely that this rite was carried out in the large central square.

from PORTA LAURENTINA to VIA DEGLI AUGUSTALI

Following the road, we reach **Porta Laurentina**, the gate in the best state of preservation, consisting of a single chamber and flanked by two square towers. After following the Cardo Maximus for less than fifty metres, the traffic coming from Porta Laurentina, especially commercial traffic heading for the Tiber and the river port, turned right into an important cross-street whose ancient name is engraved on two cippi by the sides of the road bearing the following inscription: *haec semita hor (reorum)*, ["this is the road of the warehouses"]. The road runs from south to north and is mainly flanked by commercial and industrial buildings, even after the crossroads with the Decumanus Maximus, when it becomes the Via dei Molini.

On the first stretch, on the right, you will see a warehouse from the middle of the 1st century A.D. in *opus reticulatum* and, on the opposite side of the road, a mill from the first half of the 2nd century A.D. with various types of millstones in a large columned courtyard.

Standing out from the buildings lining the road is a sumptuous upper-class dwelling. Known as the **Domus of the Protirus** because of the monumental entrance with two marble pillars supporting a pediment bearing the owners' names. The current layout dates to the beginning of the 4th century A.D. when the existing buildings underwent major remodelling.

After entering through the marble protirus, you go along a wide corridor paved with a mosaic formed of large polychrome tessarae with an elaborate nymphaeum as backdrop and a second facade overlooking an inner courtyard with a basin in the centre.

Below the basin is a small hypogeum or vault containing small wall niches and a well, thought to be a household shrine.

The large rear room, on the same axis as the entrance, is the main room or *tablinum* which originally had a pillared entrance. Around the courtyard are various *cubicula* with polychrome marble floors and black-and-white mosaic pavements.

Heading northwards, you turn right into Via della **Fortuna Annonaria** on the right side of which stands the house of the same name, a luxurious dwelling from the late Empire; the result of major restructuring which transformed an *insula* from the middle of the 2nd century A.D. into an aristocratic home.

This *domus* also has a monumental entrance with the remains of two marble columns.

A vestibule flanked by smaller rooms leads to a spacious porticoed courtyard which was already present prior to the restructuring work. Standing on a pedestal in front of the rear wall is the case of a sculpture depicting a seated

goddess with a cornucopia and an oar, identified as Fortuna Annonaria, which gave the house its name; others suggest that the statue is a personification of the city of Ostia.

Of particular interest is the main room, on your right as you enter, which opens onto a courtyard with three arches supported by slender marble pillars; a travertine dosseret rests on the capitals, an architectural solution later documented in Byzantine monuments. The room, embellished with polychrome marbles and decorated with a monumental fountain, was probably a dining room: the rear apse held the couches (the *stibadia* used in late Antiquity) on which guests would recline as they ate their meals from a semi-circular table. On the opposite side of the house are two other chambers, a larger room with a polychrome marble tile pavement, the smaller with a black-and-white patterned mosaic pavement and a heating system (the hot air tubes can still be seen in the north wall). The latter room, identified as a *cubiculum*, has a mosaic pavement with figurative motifs depicting mythological scenes and animals in alternation. Around a central octagon containing a representation of Lycurgus assailing the nymph Ambrosia, you can see: a centaur, the she-wolf with the twins, Ganymede and the eagle, a tiger, a stag, Actaeon being attacked by

his dogs, and a panther. The mosaic can be dated to the first half of the 3rd century A.D.

After you have walked almost to the end of Via della Fortuna Annonaria, you will see, on your right, the **Mithraeum of Felixissimus**, made by converting an existing building (second half of the 3rd century A.D.). As was the custom, a one did not go directly from the street into the Mithraeum but through a side room.

Although many other Ostian rooms are more imposing, this chamber is of particular significance because the stretch of mosaic pavement between the podia represents a rare document giving us information about the Mithraic cult. Two podia made of tufa blocks are situated in the inner space, while no trace remains of the altar. The entrance mosaic depicts a ritual well, a *crater* (both symbols of water), and an altar with a flame (symbol of fire). Above the *crater* are two conical caps with stars on top, a clear reference to the Dioscuri (Castor and Pollux) who, in turn, symbolised the two heavenly hemispheres. In the corridor the mosaic is divided into seven rectangular sections alluding to the seven phases of initiation and to the seven planets symbolising this mystical journey: *Corax* (Mercury); *Nymphus* (Venus); *Miles* (Mars); *Leo*

(Jupiter); *Perses* (Moon); *Heliodromus* (Sun); *Pater* (Saturn). There is an eighth section bearing an inscription with the name of the initiate who had the *Mithraeum* built: *Felicissimus ex voto f(ecit)*.

Via della Fortuna Annonaria leads us to Via degli Augustali overlooked by the **Fullonica**, or laundry and dyehouse, possibly the largest of the four *fullonicae* excavated in Ostia and undoubtedly the best-preserved.

The Fullonica we can see today was built under

Mithraeum of Felixissimus (above). **Domus of Fortuna Annonaria, statue of the betroned goddnes** (left).

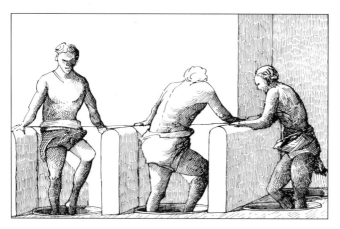

Drawing of the 'saltus fullonicus'.

Marcus Aurelius (A.D.161-180) to replace an existing one dating to the early decades of the 2nd century A.D. built on the site of a 1st-century B.C. *domus*. In the middle of this huge building divided by pillars stand a row of four vats (*lacus*) while along the walls are numerous small tubs (*pilae fullonicae*), surrounded by brick walls on which the workers leant while treading on the cloths soaking in the dyestuffs or detergents to increase the absorption of the liquids. This operation, which looked like a strange kind of dance, was known as *saltus fullonicus*. After several washes in the central vats, the cloths were hung out to dry on the terrace, of which only the stairs remain. After draining, the cloths were probably hung on joists set into sockets carved out of stone blocks set halfway up the pillars.

Fullonica of Via degli Augustali.

The last strecht of the Decumanus: from the MACELLUM to PORTA MARINA

Taberna of the Fishmonger, mosaic.

Turning left back onto the Decumanus, we pass the Forum and go as far the intersection of Via della Foce, Via degli Horrea Epagathiana and Via del Pomerio. On the left is the **Macellum**, the building used for the meat market, covering a vast trapezoidal area bounded by the Decumanus and Via del Pomerio in a very busy neighbourhood of considerable importance to local traffic. Epigraphic evidence has enabled us to piece together its history. P. Lucilius Gamala, an Ostian notable who lived during the first half of the 1st century B.C. donated a number of weights (*pondera*) to the *macellum*. A second epigraph mentions restoration taking place during the Augustan era. Later, another P. Lucilius Gamala, who lived around the middle of the 2nd century A.D., a descendent of his homonymous, more famous ancestor, emulated the latter's gesture and good works by donating further weights to the *macellum*. Finally, a last epigraphic document mentions restoration carried out by Aurelius Anicius Simmacus, a leading figure of the Senatorial aristocracy of the late Empire.

Brick and *opus mixtum* structures dating to the middle Empire make up most of the building, although the surviving pavement dates to restructuring carried out during the late Imperial age. The brick portico overlooks the crossroads; the main entrance on the Decumanus is outlined by a protirus with two Corinthian columns. Inside is a spacious square paved in marble with a fountain in the middle. The rear wall is occupied by a podium with columns, the third of which (from the left) bears an inscription that allowed the building to be identified (recently called into question by a number of experts), and reading: *lege et intellige mutu loqui ad macellum*. If the word *mutu* is interpreted as *mu(l)tu(m)*

Taberna of the Fishmonger.

the phrase means "read this and know that there is much chatter at the market"; if it is read as *mutu(m)* it must be translated as "read this and know that even a mute can speak at the market".

During the first half of the 3rd century A.D., two **Tabernae of the Fishmongers** (Taberna dei Pescivendoli) were built to either side of the main entrance, equipped with

counters and basins for the sale of fish. In the first you can see a mosaic depicting a dolphin biting an octopus with an inscription containing a popular expression against the evil eye: *inbide, te calco* ["O envious one, I tread on you"].

Walking along a brief stretch of the Decumanus, you reach the so-called **Christian Basilica**, a building dating to the end of the 4th century A.D., with an irregular plan formed of two long aisles ending in two apses. In the left-hand aisle, two columns support an architrave where you can read an inscription nominating the four rivers of the terrestrial paradise (*Geon, Tigris, Fison, Eufrata*).
The construction was identified in the past as a

The so-called 'Christian Basilica'.

THE GUILDS

During the course of the 2nd and 3rd centuries A.D., the wide range and variety of commercial and economic activities taking place in Ostia and in the Imperial ports resulted in the creation of collegia or corpora. These were professional guilds or associations that protected trade interests but whose objectives were not exclusively economic. They also carried out social functions whose precise characteristics elude us. Heading these collegiate bodies were two or three magistrates who remained in office for a five-year period, the so-called *quinquennales*, flanked by the *quaestores*, or treasurers. Among the main guilds were the *fabri tignuarii*, or constructors; the *fabri navales*, shipbuilders; *mensores frumentarii*, the official grain measurers; the *navicularii*, shipowners who were responsible for sea trade; the *pistores*, bakers; the *lenuncularii* and the *codicarii* who were responsible for river navigation using different types of boats; the *urinatores*, the divers whose main task was to salvage goods from sunken ships, and many more.

Christian basilica, but experts today believe that it may have been the seat of a heretical sect, a hostel for pilgrims or even a school for catechumens.

A short way ahead on the left is the **Schola of Trajan**, seat of the guild of *fabri navales*, one of the most important Ostian guilds which had among its members shipowners, carpenters and shipbuilders. The power of this guild, to which many leading Roman politicians belonged, lay in its control of the merchant fleet.

Built towards the middle of the 2nd century A.D. on top of an existing domus from the middle of the 1st century B.C., the building had a facade with a semi-circular exedra with recesses for fountains and *Portasanta* marble columns. Opening off the two sides of the entrance corridor are two rooms, each decorated with two columns and exedrae: the left one holds the cast of the statue of Trajan (the original location is unknown) now housed in the Museo Ostiense. The inner courtyard consists of a brick peristyle with a long central pool decorated with small internal recesses. The rear part of the building contains a series of rooms built in *opus listatum* during the 2nd century A.D. The central room, which was the banqueting hall, had an entrance with two spiral columns and was embellished with a mosaic depicting winged genies and animals surrounded by vegetal decorations. In the eastern sector of the courtyard, you can see the structures of one of the preceding 1st-century B.C. domus that have been left on

view and reconstructed on a raised area: they consist of a peristyle with brick columns whose ambulatory pavement is formed of a mosaic with white tesserae on a black background, and another room with walls in *opus reticulatum* and a fine geometrically patterned mosaic pavement.

On the opposite side of the Decumanus, is the **Temple of the Fabri Navales**, the place of worship for this guild and obviously very closely linked to the *Schola*. Built towards the end of the 2nd century A.D., the complex consists of a large rectangular courtyard surrounded by a brick-pillared portico to the rear of which the temple stands. In the north-western corner is the plinth of a statue with an inscription mentioning Flavius Filippus, patron of the *fabri navales*, which allowed the edifice to be identified.

Stacked up in the courtyard are plinths and capitals as well as numerous Greek marble columns some of which bearing the name *Volusianus*, which may refer to C. *Ceionius Rufus Volusianus Lampadius*, who was *praetor urbanus* or town magistrate from A.D. 365-66 and wealthy entrepreneur. It is therefore likely that during the late Empire the building was used as a marble depot and workshop.

Returning to the Decumanus, we will now walk down the entire road to the **Porta Marina**, situated

Temple of the Fabri Navales.

near to the ancient beach (around 150 m). Now at a lower level with respect to the Imperial era, it consists of a single structure with masonry made of tufa blocks in *opus quadratus* flanked by two outer towers. The imposing nature of the structure may result from the vulnerability of the side facing the beach to maritime attacks, as shown by the A.D. 67 raid by Cilician pirates (just a few years before the wall was built) and the episode of defence of Ostia's coast depicted in the relief on the sepulchre of Cartilius Poplicola (in Route 7).

the EXTRA-URBAN QUARTER outside PORTA MARINA

During the last decades of the 1st century B.C., two funerary monuments were built in an open space extending from the walls to the sea. From the first century of the Empire onwards, this space began to turn into a built-up area, although its layout did not become definitive until the 2nd century A.D., and the high point of its expansion was not reached until the late Empire. The underlying reasons for this phenomenon, which was unique to this area of Ostia, are not only the vicinity to the sea, which was overlooked by the most important and luxurious buildings, but also the presence of the nearby Via Severana, the vital coastal route linking the town of Portus to Antium. However, even at the height of the Imperial age, the two late-Republican sepulchres, evidently intended to perpetuate the memory of famous personages, were respected and their original form left untouched.

On the right, immediately after the gate, is the first **Funerary Monument** of which only the lower part consisting of a concrete core

Large buildings near Porta Marina.

faced with carved travertine blocks still survives. Of particular interest is the east-facing front which forms a rectangular exedra containing seats decorated with lion's paws and dolphins. An enclosure with side walls made of tufa blocks and travertine fronts with semi-circular exedrae was added during a later phase. The study of the many architectural fragments found during the course of the excavations have permitted an ideal reconstruction to be developed: on top of the basis stood a cylindrical body with columns (*tholos*) and a

continuous entablature formed of an architrave, frieze and cornice covered by a conical roof with scale decorations. The monument was probably built around 40-30 B.C.

On the opposite side is a large area known as the Forum of Porta Marina, dating to the reign of Hadrian, formed by an almost square colonnaded space whose original purpose is uncertain: possibly a halting place for coastal traffic or, more probably, a place of worship. The presence of a kind of altar and the discovery of fragments of an inscription referring to the cult of Vulcan make the latter hypothesis more likely.

After continuing along the Decumanus, we turn left into Via di Cartilio, at the beginning of which is the **Sepulchre of C. Cartilius Poplicola** which dates to the late Republican era. Far older than the other buildings in the area, it obviously lies below the level of the street. The monument has a square plan with a core in *opus caementicium* faced with marble blocks. A central body with a lower cornice and side pilasters stands on a travertine base. Only the front has been reconstructed by putting together the architectural elements discovered during the excavations. The middle section contains an inscription referring to the person to whom the sepulchre was dedicated, and on the top left and right are eight lictor fasces, symbols of civil authority referring to the

eight occasions on which this personage was elected to the duovirate, the town's highest magisterial office.

Above the dado is a figurative relief characterised by the fairly simple almost rough style that distinguished Italic art, a far cry from the Hellenistic trend that was so popular in Rome at the time and depicting, on the right, a trireme of soldiers engaged in a naval battle and, on the left, other soldiers in tunics and carrying shields lined up on the terra firma. The scene describes a military operation that took place in two phases – a naval battle, followed by the arrayment of foot soldiers on shore after the landing – and may refer to a pirate raid on the Ostian coast, defended by a small troop of soldiers led by Cartilius Poplicola. The precise historical episode on which it is based, and to which the glory and popularity of this notable can be traced, remains unknown. We do know, however, that

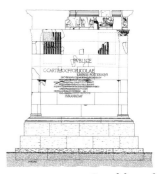

Sepulchre of Cartilius Poplicola, drawing reconstructing the front.

the sepulchre was located close to the sea in commemoration of this event, and that it was decorated with rostra with triple-ribbed rams (one of which also decorates Porta Marina's other mausoleum) for the same reason. Important facts about the public life of this personality can be inferred from the inscription on the facade: *Pu [bli] ce / [C (aio) Carti] li [o C(ai) f(ilio) Pop] licolae [-- -- --] / [-- -- --] libereis pos [terisque] eius / [decurionum decreto co] lonorumque con [sensu] / preimario viro pro eius meritieis / hoc [m] on umentum constitutum est / eique merenti gratia rellata est / isque octiens duomvir, ter cens(or) colonorum iudicio / apsens praesensque factus est / ob eius amorem in universos ab / universieis... / Humaniae M(arci) f(iliae)* ["This monument was erected at public expense. To Caius Cartilius Poplicola son of Caius... and to his sons and descendants by decree of the decurions and with the consent of the colonists this monument has been dedicated to him,

---

THE CITY ADMINISTRATION

During the Republican period, Ostia, like the other Roman colonies, was governed by *two praetores* or *magistrates* and was subjected to strict administrative control on the part of Rome. However, after the social war, at the beginning of the 1st century A.D., institutional changes took place, establishing new criteria for municipal administration. The city was subsequently governed by two *magistrates* who remained in office for one year, the so-called *duoviri*. Every five years they drew up a new register for the city council, taking the title of *duoviri quinquennales* for the occasion.

Under the *duoviri* were two *aediles*, the *officials* responsible for the organisation of public services (roads, baths, etc.). Finally, there was a *quaestor* who was responsible for financial administration. The City Council was formed of 100 members, called *decuriones*, elected every five years.

Baths of Porta Marina, mosaic pavement.

distinguished by merits and recipient of well-deserved commendations. He was elected duovir eight times and censor three times, both in his presence and in his absence. For the love he showed to everyone… To Humania Daughter of Marcus"].

Cartilius Poplicola was one of the most important Ostian

Synagogue.

personages between the end of the Republican age and the first decades of the Augustan era. So great was his popularity that the citizenry awarded him the honorary surname *Poplicola* ("friend of the people"). His political career was a very long one, covering a time span from the last three or four decades of the 1st century B.C. to the beginning of the 1st century A.D. He was elected as duovir, the city's highest magisterial office, no less than eight times, on three of these occasions also holding the office of *Censor* (responsible for assessing the register of the citizen's council).

Standing a short distance away are the imposing **Baths of Porta Marina** (or 'of the Marciana'), Ostia's third largest complex of *thermae*. The ancient name of these baths was *thermae maritimae*, and is contained in an inscription now housed in the Capitoline Museums. Construction began under Trajan and it is to this phase

that the marble head of Marciana, the Emperor's sister, who gave the edifice its second name, dates. Finished around the middle of the 2nd century A.D., during the Imperial age, the building underwent restoration on various occasions up to the 6th century, an indication of the continuing vitality of this extra-urban quarter even during the later epoch (unlike the rest of Ostia, practically abandoned by this time) resulting from its link by means of the Via Severana to the commercial and economic activities of Portus. The building consists of a gymnasium (originally colonnaded) and the thermal baths (on a raised floor). The baths were reached via two side entrances each equipped with a small staircase and ramp. In the *apodyterium* is a 3rd-century A.D. mosaic depicting athletes around a table with prizes. The *frigidarium*, with its lovely late polychrome mosaic from the 4th-5th

century A.D. contains a swimming pool with apse (added in the 3rd century A.D.) and large brick pillars that must have supported the vault.

The two end rooms on the eastern side communicating with the gymnasium have pavement mosaics decorated with marine scenes from the middle of the 3rd century A.D.. The southern part contains the heated *caldarium* and two *tepidaria* (from west to east).

East of the baths a path leads to the Synagogue, where Ostia's flourishing Jewish community met. Alongside is the basalt road surface of the Via Severana. Probably dating to the beginning of the 1st century A.D., the original temple was completely rebuilt in *opus listatum* during the 4th century A.D. A narthex leads into the building which basically consists of two large rooms.

The northern room is a hall with four high columns by the entrance; in one corner is a tabernacle flanked by two small pillars supporting corbels depicting seven-branched candelabra (*menorah*); it faced south-east towards Jerusalem and was considered the most holy place where the scroll of the laws was kept (*Torah*). The other chamber, in the south, may have been used for meetings. There is also another room with an oven and a marble bench where dough was kneaded.

the QUARTER by VIA DELLA FOCE

Temple of Hercules.

Going back through Porta Marina along the Decumanus, we reach a crossing with Via della Foce (road of the river-mouth) which, as the modern name suggests, led to the mouth of the Tiber, following what is possibly Ostia's oldest road route. Overlooking the road, set at a lower level than the Imperial-age basalt paving, is the **Republican Sanctuary**, the city's largest sacred monumental complex.

The entire area is dominated by the mass of the main temple dating to the end of the 2nd - beginning of the 1st century B.C. and dedicated to Hercules. There is a high podium with a wide front stair; it originally had six columns on the front and three along the sides of the pronaos. In the cella we can see the scarce remains of the original masonry in *opus quasi-reticulatum* and some stretches of wall in *opus mixtum* built during subsequent restoration in the early 2nd century A.D.

The cult of Hercules had an oracular character in Ostia, demonstrated by the cast of a relief (the original is in the museum) found near the temple and now mounted on the wall of the adjoining building. The episode is divided into three scenes: the statue of an armed Hercules being miraculously fished out of the water; the god taking an oracle from a casket and handing it to an acolyte of the cult; finally, a *haruspex* (an augur who foretold the future by examining the entrails of sacrificed animals) who is passing it to another figure over whom Victory is flying. It can be interpreted as the fortunate consultation of the oracle by the commander of a fleet about to leave for a military expedition. It has been pointed out that not far from the sanctuary was the sector of the river port

reserved for war-ships. The relief also contains an inscription with the name of the donor: *C. Fulvius haruspex d(onum) d(edit)* ["This relief was dedicated by the *haruspex* Caius Fluvius"]. It is dated to the 80-60 B.C. period.

Standing in the pronaos is the cast (the original is in the museum) of a male statue portraying 'the hero at rest', a votive gift dedicated by Cartilius Poplicola, Ostia's leading political figure at the end of the 1st century B.C., and defender of the city during various attacks, recalled in the sepulchre dedicated to him just outside Porta Marina. Engraved on the plinth is the following inscription: *C. Cartilius C(ai) f(ilius) duoviru tertio Poplicolae*

Baths of the Seven Sages, *frigidarium*, room with polychrome wall mosaic.

["Caius Cartilius made this donation when he became duovir for the third time. To Poplicola"]. The surname *Poplicola* (which means "friend of the people") is written with the wrong grammatical ending and was added at a later date, maybe to emphasise the outstanding merits of this personage.

In the pronaos is an altar with a dedication to Hercules, described as Hercules Invictus, on the part of Ostilius Antipatrus, Prefect of the Annona at the end of the 3rd century B.C. The cult obviously continued throughout the Imperial age: another inscription informs us that, during the final years of the 4th century B.C., when Christianity had become well-established, the temple was restored by the Prefect of the Annona, Numerius Proiectus. This probably represented the very last occasion on which a sacred pagan edifice was restored by the public authorities of Rome; further proof of the persistence of traditional rites in Ostia.

On the northern side of the sacred area is the **Tetrastyle Temple** (end of 2nd century B.C.) whose name derives from the four tufa columns on the front. It is built in *opus incertum* on a tufa podium, like the columns of the pronaos crowned by peperino Corinthian capitals. The discovery of a Hellenistic-age torso of Asclepius during excavations suggests that it may have dedicated to this divinity.

The third edifice, called the **Temple of the Round Altar** (Tempio dell'Ara Rotonda) following the discovery of a circular altar, is situated below Via della Foce and is almost concealed by the Temple of Hercules. It is not easy to interpret or identify the purpose of the structures. There were two construction phases, one dating to the Republican age (1st century B.C.) and the second to the Imperial era (end of 1st century A.D.). Originally with a tufa podium and side entrance, the edifice was later enlarged and rebuilt in brick masonry on a higher level, becoming a dystyle temple (that is with two columns on the facade) with a front entrance. The construction of the new foundations re-used the travertine plinths of statues (now housed in the museum) with inscriptions bearing the names of Greek artists, relative to Greek works of art used to decorate the sanctuary during its earlier phase (1st century B.C.). We now walk along Via della

---

RELIGIOUS LIFE: THE MAIN CULTS

Among the divinities of the traditional religion, particular veneration was reserved for the Dioscuri (Castor and Pollux), who were the protectors of navigation, and for Hercules, whose sanctuary near the military port was visited by sailors and commanders of fleets. However, one numen was worshipped more than any other: Vulcan, the fire god, whose importance stems from the fact that this cult was introduced by the very first Roman colonists at the time of Ostia's foundation (620 B.C.). The highest sacerdotal authority, the *Pontifex Vulcani*, was elected by the Pontifex Maximus of Rome, and was responsible for overseeing all the other Ostian cults. The dedication of an altar or statues in the sanctuaries or the construction of temples of other divinities had to be authorised by him.

Insula of the Charioteers, inner courtyard.

Foce for a short stretch as far as the monumental complex formed by the Insula of Serapis, the Baths of the Seven Sages and the Insula of the Charioteers, an emblematic example of residential housing during the height of the Imperial age. The complex is formed of two buildings with porticoed courtyards joined by a common thermal building designed and built under Hadrian.

The **Insula of Serapis**, which you enter from Via della Foce, takes its name from the portrait of Serapis (Severan period, stucco) set in an aedicule in the courtyard containing brick pillars going up to the level of the first-floor ceiling and surrounded by small rooms like *tabernae*. The apartments must have been situated on the upper floors, reached via staircases going from the ambulatory of the

central courtyard. Passing through a doorway with stucco decorations, you enter the **Baths of the Seven Sages** (Terme dei Sette Sapienti), which may date to Hadrian's reign. A vestibule leads to the circular *frigidarium*, originally covered with a dome, containing a striking mosaic with an intricate pattern of vegetal motifs and hunting scenes. In the north wall, a recess with a wall mosaic leads to the changing-rooms which, before becoming part of the bath complex, was an inn. This room contains ironic depictions of the Seven Sages (Solomon, Thales, etc.) illustrated by phrases jokingly attributed to them containing, not philosophical maxims, but advice about how to ensure a healthily functioning intestine. A short way ahead, on the right, is a second *frigidarium* with a beautiful painting of *Aphrodite Anadiomene* (that is emerging from the waters) on the rear wall. On the opposite side, there is a corridor followed by two *tepidaria* - the second of which has an attractive mosaic with marine scenes - and a *caldarium* with two pools.

We now enter the **Insula of the Charioteers** or Caseggiato degli Aurighi (dating to around 140 A.D.) which consists of the usual arcaded courtyard with an ambulatory running around it, on the north side of which are two interesting

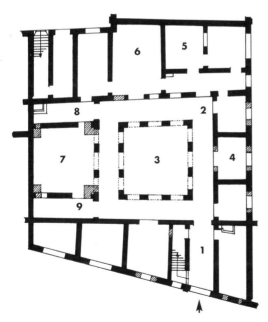

Fig. 8. Insula of the Muses.
1 Entrance; 2 Corridor;
3 Courtyard; 4 Living Room; 5 *Cubiculum*; 6 *Triclinium*;
7 *Tablinum*; 8 and 9 open rooms (*alae*).

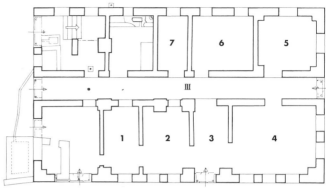

**Fig. 9. Insula of the Painted Vaults.
1-4 rooms with paintings with yellow backgrounds;
5 room with painting with white background.**

**Frescoes from the
Insula of the Muses.**

pictures depicting two charioteers in bigae (two-horse chariots). The apartment on the right side of the corridor is decorated with particularly fine paintings consisting of panels containing depictions of cupids, still lifes and scenes of stag and panther hunts. The surviving

building structure reaches a height of around ten metres, as far as the impost of the third-floor vault. The *insula* may have been rented to a number of tenants or possibly reserved for some sporting guild, as the pictures of the charioteers may suggest. Leaving the Insula of the Charioteers, enter Via degli Aurighi then turn right into Vico delle Volte Dipinte where you will find the **Insula of the Muses** (Fig. 8 on previous page). The edifice (dating to

the reign of Hadrian - A.D. 128) with its porticoed courtyard belongs to a building category frequently encountered in Ostia and often used for the large multi-storeyed apartment blocks. In this case, however, this type of structure was used for a sumptuous two-storeyed house inhabited by one family undoubtedly belonging to the wealthy middle-class, reflected in its harmonious layout.

For example, it has been discovered that the pictorial decoration of the rooms took into account the exposure to light. Consequently, clear bright colours were used to paint the shady rooms to create a sensation of light and spaciousness; while strong, dark colours were used for the rooms with large apertures.

To enter the house you pass through a vestibule flanked, on the left, by a stair leading to the upper floor, and on the right, by the kitchen. On the right,

Insula of the Painted Vaults, vault frescoes.

Insula of the Painted Vaults, central corridor.

you go along the courtyard corridor of which the various rooms open. The first is a *cubiculum*; the second an oecus, that is a small drawing room (Room 4), whose walls are decorated by a pictorial cycle depicting Apollo and the nine Muses within square panels separated by delicate architectural elements, dominated by warm red and yellow backgrounds. This mural painting is of great importance because it provides a testimony of post-Pompeian pictorial art and a confirmation that, even fifty years after the destruction of Pompei and Herculaneum, the tendency to use scenery and false architecture still persisted, although to a lesser extent. The next room is another *cubiculum*.

The first two rooms in the northern side, more isolated and quiet, were the owner's quarters: one has an attractive floor mosaic, the other (the *cubiculum* -

Room 5) has walls painted with delicate architectural motifs and Dionysian figures against a white background. The next large room is a *triclinium* (Room 6) embellished with remarkable mural paintings depicting columns, pilasters, balconies and even an open door through which female figures are passing. On the lower part of the southern wall is a section of painting dating to a later period (first half of the 4th century A.D.) with a painted marble effect.

On the western side is the largest room, communicating with the courtyard by means of arches on pilasters, flanked by open rooms (alae, 8-9) and recalling the tablinum of the Pompeian *domus*, that is the most important solemn room in the whole house (Room 7). The walls of the eastern ala are decorated by paintings with delicate vegetal and animal motifs on white backgrounds separated by slender architectural

elements. Another fresco in the same corridor contains a number of graffiti of which the most interesting is a drawing of Trajan's Column by a Greek who signs himself *Hieron*.

On the other side of the street is the **Insula of the Painted Vaults** (Insula delle Volte Dipinte) dating to A.D. 120 (Fig. 9), a house with an extremely unusual plan, resembling in many respects that of modern homes. It consists of a long central corridor off which the various rooms open, to the left and right. It lacks the usual courtyard and the only source of light is represented by the external windows with which all the rooms are supplied. The first floor has partially survived with its outside stairs. This *insula* is famous for its remarkable decorations which not only consist of mural paintings but also of partially preserved vault paintings, a find outstanding for its rarity. The frescoes were carried out during five different periods; the best documented phase dates to the Antonine age and was partially inspired by the iconographic models in vogue at the end of the 1st century A.D. These paintings basically belong to two styles: the first, with prevalently yellow and red backgrounds, has architectural (columns, porticoes), geometrical and figurative (human and animal figures) motifs using a rich chromatic palette and characterising the reception

Garden Apartments, aerial view.

rooms (Rooms 1-5). The second, with white backgrounds, has schematised decorative and architectural motifs using a narrower colour range (mainly red, green and yellow) and is used for the private rooms (Bedrooms 6-7). Even the ceiling decorations use the same styles and colours as the mural paintings, without interruptions, using layouts with central medallions, strips and squares also defined by the ribbing of the cross-vaults. Dating to the Severan age is the redecoration of one of the ceilings (Room 5) with a central tondo containing winged horse and rider and lunettes with stock scenes (birds, pigmies, etc.). The erotic picture in Room 6 belongs to a later phase (around A.D. 240) and is probably linked to the use of this particular room and not, as some have suggested, to a rather unlikely transformation of the house into a brothel. During the same period, a corner room, which may have originally been an open loggia, was transformed into a bar and a counter was added. The original decorations in popular style (from the Antonine era) which may have represented a funerary rite in honour of the departed, portrayed in a tondo, were left unchanged.

Continuing along Via delle Volte Dipinte we turn right where there is an open space containing the **Insula of the Yellow Walls** (Insula delle Pareti Gialle), another high-class two-storey residence with reception rooms on the ground floor. The rectangular floor plan contains a central space onto which the other rooms face, with large windows to allow light into the inner rooms. The edifice, built under Hadrian, contains successive pictorial phases that confirm the continuous reconstructions undergone by the building until around the middle of the 3rd century A.D. The most well-represented is the phase dating to the Antonine era (A.D. 180-190) characterised by a prevalent use of yellow (giving the house its name), constantly combined with red. The layouts use architectural motifs, with pilasters or aedicules alternating with panels containing small squares decorated with buildings or landscapes painted using swift brush-strokes. A similar layout is used for the walls attributed to the first half of the 3rd century, ending with the reduction of the aedicule to skeletal linear elements. One of the rooms contains a more recent decoration, a mythological painting depicting the battle between Hercules and Achelous possibly inspired by a work from the Hellenistic era. This room was redecorated during a later period with mural paintings of fake marble facing with geometrical motifs.

Going ahead on the right, we reach the **Garden Apartments** (Case Giardino), which originally had a monumental entrance flanked by brick pillars on Via degli Aurighi. A trapezoidal urban site is occupied by this rectangular complex, formed of several insulae of various depths, designed and built during the Hadrianic era.

Baths of Mithra, *mithraeum*.

The living units on this site are surrounded by a garden area with six fountains. The multi-storey *insulae* are grouped into two blocks, both with central covered passage-ways, in the centre of an open space. These luxurious apartments, reserved for middle-class tenants, had no ground-floor *tabernae*. Traces of the mural decorations still remain.

From the east side of the garden we can enter the **Domus of the Dioscuri** (although the real apsidal entrance is on the nearby Vico dei Dipinti). The building as it appears today was built during late Antiquity by transforming a 2nd-century A.D. house and completely changing its structure.

The two main rooms open off the end of an L-shaped corridor. The first, to the south, is a bedroom decorated with a polychrome mosaic with an octagonal pattern, at the centre of which the Dioscuri are depicted. As the protectors of trade, the Heavenly Twins were the object of particular veneration in Ostia. The second room is a spacious hall containing another outstanding polychrome mosaic stylistically inspired by African models, depicting Venus in a shell among dolphins, maenads and monsters. The south side of the room leads to two *cubicula*. The first contains a floor mosaic with the letters "PE" flanked by a palm, thought to be an allusion to the Apostle Peter. The second *cubiculum* contains a polychrome mosaic with a geometrical pattern. In the western sector are small baths with a *frigidarium*, *caldarium* and *tepidarium*, the only private bathing facility known in Ostia.

It has been suggested that the owner of the house was a shipowner or merchant who made his fortune importing grain from Africa. A more likely hypothesis is that the *domus* belonged to Ceionius Rufus Volusianus, the owner of a marble workshop in the nearby temple of the *fabri navales* and *praetor urbanus* from A.D. 365-66 who was required to attend the annual Ostian feast of the Dioscuri in his official capacity.

After going back as far as Via della Foce, we turn into Via delle Terme di Mitra, the site of the **Baths of Mithras** (Terme del Mitra) built during Hadrian's reign. We enter the baths through a side entrance and pass through a number of service areas including, on the left, a narrow space where the hydraulic wheel (*noria*) was originally located. The baths consist of the following rooms (going from south to

Domus of Cupid and Psyche.

north): *caldarium* with two pools; *frigidarium* with one apsidal pool; an access area with two Corinthian columns by the northern entrance, decorated with a floor mosaic depicting Ulysses and the Sirens; finally, a room restructured during the late Empire for the purposes of the Christian cult, with an apse in the rear and a kind of presbytery in the central part. A stair in the north-eastern corner leads to an underground service room that was later converted into a Mithraeum. In the rear stands a marble group of Mithras killing the bull (the original is in the museum) lit by a skylight in an extremely evocative atmosphere. When the baths were converted to create spaces for the Christian cult, the sculpture was hacked to pieces and thrown into a sewer. The fragments where later rediscovered and put back together again.

Going back to Via della Foce, we walk as far as the sacred Republican area, where we take a path running behind the back wall of the Temple of Hercules. On the left is the **Domus of Cupid and Psyche**, another sumptuous home from the late Empire (second half of the 3rd century A.D.). This house, which may have been used as a summer residence, was

Horrea Epagathiana, entrance portal.

quiet and set aside, or rather, almost concealed from the nearby buildings.

A small entrance leads to the corridor whose left side is formed by an arcaded facade (only partially preserved) with slender columns. On the other side is a small garden containing a nymphaeum with niches from which water poured. At the end of the corridor is the *triclinium* which stands out for its beautiful *opus sectile* pavement and the marble wall facings.

Opening off the west side of the corridor are three small rooms. Remains of a refined *opus sectile* pavement and marble facings testify to the elegance of the middle room which also contains the marble group that gave the *domus* its name.

Walking right to the end of the path you will find the building known as **Horrea Epagathiana** built in the middle of the 2nd century A.D. The impressive brick portal is formed of two semi-columns surmounted by an architrave and tympanum.
The inscription on the architrave informs us of the building's function as well as the identity of its owners: *horrea Epagathiana et Epaphroditiana* ["the warehouses of Epagathus and Epaphroditus"].
From the presence of two entrance doors and of other doors in the inner courtyard leading to the stairs to the upper floors we can deduce that these warehouses may have been used to store precious goods (like cloths, furniture, etc.).

The building belonged to two freedmen of eastern origin (as their names suggest), who had become rich through trade; a frequent occurrence during the Imperial age.

It belongs to the category of building with a central porticoed courtyard, which, as we saw earlier with regard to the *insulae*, is particularly well-documented in Ostia. Interestingly, widespread use was made of this feature during the Renaissance, on a more monumental scale, for cloisters and palazzi.

The courtyard pavement is decorated with a mosaic with depictions of a tiger and panther together with geometrical motifs.
On the ground floor are sixteen vaulted rooms which were the actual storage cells; the first and second floors (of which the first steps of another stair survive) may have been used for storage or for the owners' quarters.

ALAE: in the Roman houses, small rooms with side apertures in the atrium without any precise function. During earlier times, when the atrium was roofed, they may have been intended to let light and air into the home.

APODYTERIUM: changing-rooms in the thermae, furnished with long benches along the walls and deep recesses in the wall where clothes could be placed.

ATRIUM: the central area of the front part of the Roman house during the Republican age off which the bedrooms (see *cubicula*) opened. It generally had an uncovered central space with a rain-water tank (see *impluvium*).

CALDARIUM: room in the thermae for hot baths with one or more pools. The room was heated by hot air passing through cavities in the walls and below the floor which was raised on small pillars (see *suspensurae*).

CELLA: generic term for rooms with various functions: for example, the room of a temple which contained a statue of the divinity, rooms for the storage of grain or other foodstuffs, etc.

COLUMBARIUM: sepulchral chamber lined with recesses for urns containing the ashes of those who have been cremated. The name derives from its resemblance to a dovecot.

CRATER (latin: *creterre*): large two-handled bowl used for mixing wine and water in a given proportion. The water-down wine was scooped up using a smaller receptacle.

CYMBALUM: percussion instrument formed of two bronze disks.

DECUMANUS: the road axis running from east to west in Roman towns.

DOLIUM: large pot-bellied container with a 1000/2000-litre capacity used for storing wine, oil or other foodstuffs (grain, pulses, etc.).

DOMUS (house): elegant single-family home widely used during the Republican age and the first century of the Imperial age. Usually single-storeyed, with rooms facing onto the *atrium* (see) and onto the porticoed garden (see *peristylium*).

EMBLEMA (emblem): central decoration of a pavement generally consisting of a mosaic made of minute tesserae with a figurative depiction.

EXHEDRA (exedra): in public and private buildings, semi-circular or rectangular recess with an open front.

FRIGIDARIUM: room in the thermae for cold baths with one or more pools.

GENS (family): group of families who, either because of male descendancy or by birth, adoption or marriage, have a common male ancestor whose name (*gentilicium nomen*) they bear. They shared the same family divinity and religious and funerary rites, a spirit of solidarity and mutual assistance, and attended family meetings.

HORREA (warehouses): large warehouses used for storage of goods and foodstuffs. They were known as horrea granaria if used for grain which was stored inside *cellae* (see) with a loose stone foundation under the floor to prevent rising damp.

INSULA ("island"): multi-storeyed (up to four or five floors) apartment block with stairs and balconies, and shops on ground floor. It was originally set apart from other building complexes, creating a kind of island.

LACONICUM: fairly small, elliptical or circular room in the thermae for sweat-baths. It had a small aperture in the centre of vault and was heated by hot air piped through the wall cavities and under the floor.

NARTHEX: portico supported by columns or pillars on the facade of the ancient Christian basilicas, reserved for penitents or catachumens.

Baths of the Seven Sages, *frigidarium* (left).

NAVE: the space between the two central rows of roof supports in a hall whose roof is supported by pillars.

NYMPHAEUM: fountain, more or less monumental, often decorated with niches and columns.

OECUS: In the Roman house, a kind of living room or reception chamber without any precise function.

OPUS INCERTUM (irregular exposed stonework): wall facing formed of small rough-cast stones with irregular edges.
Widely used during the 2nd century A.D.

OPUS LATERICIUM (brickwork): wall facing formed of bricks.
Sporadically used during the 1st century A.D., it was most extensively used between the middle of the 2nd and the middle of the 3rd centuries A.D.

OPUS LISTATUM or VITTATUM (exposed stripwork): wall facing formed of alternating rows of tufa stone and bands of brickwork.
Widely used from the middle of the 3rd century A.D. onwards.

OPUS QUADRATUM (dry intersecting masonry): masonry made from large squared blocks of tufa or travertine, mainly used during the archaic and Republican ages.

OPUS QUASI RETICULATUM (irregular exposed stonework): wall facing formed of tufa (or stone) rhomboids creating an irregular wavy reticulate pattern. Mainly used during the first half of the 1st century A.D.

OPUS RETICULATUM (regular exposed stonework): wall facing formed of tufa (or stone) laid in oblique lines creating a regular reticulate pattern. Mainly used from the end of the 1st century A.D. and for most of the 2nd century A.D.

OPUS SECTILE: type of wall mosaic or facing using polychrome marble fragments to compose geometrical motifs.

ORCHESTRA: In the Greek theatre, circular space for the choir. In Roman times it became semi-circular in shape.

PARADOS: side corridor leading to stage in theatre.

PERISTILIUM (peristyle): colonnade surrounding a central space, usu. garden or courtyard.

POPINA (tavern): popular inn where beverages, foods and ready meals were sold.

PRONAOS: in the Classical period, the porticoed area in front of the cella.

PROTIRUS: entrance, more or less monumental, with portico supported by columns or pilasters.

QUADRIPORTICO: portico surrounding a square or rectangular central space.

SUSPENSURAE: brick columns supporting the floors of the heated rooms in the thermae allowing the hot air to circulate.

TABERNA: generic term for shop or inn.

TABLINUM: in the Roman house, reception chamber situated between the *atrium* (see) and *peristilium* (see). During ancient times, the residence of the head of the family and place where the family met.

TEPIDARIUM: warm room in the thermae heated by hot air distributed through wall cavities.

TETRASTYLE: building, usu. temple, with a four columned facade.

THERMOPOLIUM: literally, inn where warm drinks were sold.

BIBLIOGRAPHY

Main texts available in bookshops or libraries

Meiggs, R. *Roman Ostia,* Oxford 1973 (2nd ed.).

Pavolini, C. *Ostia* (Laterza archeological guidebooks), Rome 1983.

Various authors, *'Roman Ostia' revisited,* Rome 1996.

'Scavi di Ostia' series

Calza, G., Becatti, G., Gismondi, I., De Angelis D'Ossat, G., Bloch, H, I, *Topografia Generale,* Rome 1953.

Becatti, G., II, *I mitrei,* Rome 1954.

Floriani Squarciapino, M. (Ed.), III, *Le necropoli republicane ed augustee,* Rome 1958.

Calza, R., V, *I ritratti,* Rome 1964.

Becatti, G., VI, *Edificio con opus sectile fuori Porta Marina,* Rome 1969.

Pensabene, P., VII, *I capitelli,* Rome 1973.

Pietrogrande, A. L., VIII, *Le fulloniche,* Rome 1976.

Baccini Leotardi, P., IX, *Marmi di cava rinvenuti a Ostia e considerazioni sul commercio dei marmi in età romana,* Rome 1979.

Cicerchia, P., Marinucci, A., XI, *Le terme del Foro o di Gavio Massimo,* Rome 1992.

Paroli, L., (Ed.), XII, *La basilica cristiana di Pianabella,* Rome 1999.

Pavolini, C., XIII, *La ceramica comune. Le forme in argilla depurata dell'antiquarium,* Rome 2000.

Printed in July 2000
By Industrie Poligrafiche Friulane,
Pordenone, Italy.